AF652213

SHAKESPEARE
AND
DONNE

Themes of Love, Time and Mutability

SHAKESPEARE AND DONNE

Themes of Love, Time and Mutability

R. Thangvunga

ATLANTIC
PUBLISHERS & DISTRIBUTORS (P) LTD

Published by
ATLANTIC
PUBLISHERS & DISTRIBUTORS (P) LTD
7/22, Ansari Road, Darya Ganj,
New Delhi-110002
Phones : +91-11-40775252, 23273880, 23275880, 23280451
Fax : 91-11-23285873
Web : www.atlanticbooks.com
E-mail : orders@atlanticbooks.com

Branch Office
5, Nallathambi Street, Wallajah Road,
Chennai-600002
Phones : +91-44-64611085, 32413319
E-mail : chennai@atlanticbooks.com

Copyright © The Author, 2010

ISBN 978-81-269-1399-2

All rights reserved. No part of this publication may be reproduced, stored in a retrieval system, transmitted or utilized in any form or by any means, electronic, mechanical, photocopying, recording or otherwise, without the prior permission of the copyright owner. Application for such permission should be addressed to the publisher.

Printed in India at Nice Printing Press, A-33/3A, Site-IV, Industrial Area, Sahibabad, Ghaziabad, U.P.

To the memory of
my grandmother
Laltei
(1889-1969)

Preface

To most Shakespearean scholars the subject of this book is not only familiar but overworked. But to say that the topic is exhausted is a near blasphemy. The quality of a work is adjudged not by its limitations but by its undiminished interest. A familiar landscape has in store enough mystery and truth to outlast mankind. Similar is the nature of literary masterpieces so that increase of knowledge, heightened sensibilities, sharper intelligence, and richer spiritual experience yield ever more rewarding study. Every age and every generation has its peculiar taste and specific need. Not only Shakespeare, but all great artists wear the chameleon skin that suits the "very age and body of the time".

Our age, which has much affinity with what Shakespeare and Donne knew and expressed in their work, is in the grip of relentless economic forces which dehumanize people and transform essential values into commodities. Modern man, like in Caesar's Rome, scrambles for a fitful existence among the rubbles of war and waste. Scepticism and loss of faith in man's innate goodness disintegrates the very fabric of human co-existence, bringing forth senseless violence and meaningless suffering to millions. Man needs salvation, if not from outside, at least from inside. Shakespeare and Donne show that man needs the unity of his entire being—spirit, mind and body—to attain his salvation, this side of the grave.

A great adventure like the present study always humbles one; the experience and knowledge gained belittle one, and effect a kind of catharsis. It is my pleasure to offer this book to students and teachers in the hope that a waning interest in Shakespeare and Donne might be revived, and their faith in man renewed and strengthened to create a fresh will in life and work.

R. Thangvunga

Contents

1

Introduction

Time watches from the shadow
And coughs when you would kiss.

W.H. Auden

More than in any previous age, it was during the Renaissance that man became truly conscious of his inner potential and of an existential situation enveloping him. While the inner potential was his exciting possession that meant to be worked out in the best possible way and on the largest possible canvas, the outer existential situation, understood in terms of time and space, i.e. of temporal and spatial circumstances more often than not pressed upon him as a limiting, frustrating, even a maddeningly agonizing factor over which he had hardly any control. Thus, even as he became aware of the power of awakening that love brought him, he could not remain insensitive to the destructive power of time and circumstances. Love's ebullient strength, he was anguished to realize, lay at the mercy of time and change. Indeed, never before in human history did man feel so cheated of his dues, never before did he hear the winged chariot of time hurrying near as menacingly. And never before did he cry out as plangently.

Love is one of the most powerful themes in Shakespeare's plays and poems and can be seen as the real motor of some of his creations. And Donne is pre-eminently the poet of love. As Renaissance artists, both were haunted by the frightening awareness of time's destruction. They show, among other things, what chances Love has under the tyranny of Time.

An exploration of the theme of Love, Time and Mutability in the works of Shakespeare and Donne could be of absorbing interest. We are conscious of the extensive range scholarship available to us in the field. While we will naturally draw heavily on the existing scholarship, we will not fail to make our own individual explorations of the texts and we may be able, in the process, to bring some touch of freshness to our understanding of these two great authors in their distinctly individual treatments of love and time in the face of the ineluctable force of change known as Mutability.

Definitive questions on Love, Time and Mutability, though vital, need not take us into a philosophical Augean stable. It would not even be appropriate to treat them as philosophical concepts here any more than we should expect Shakespeare and Donne to write their poems and plays as philosophical works. Shakespeare was a professional playwright, and Donne rendered into poetry thoughts and feelings which others would confide in personal diaries. But they were not less alive to the scientific and philosophical novelties of their day than we are to the happenings across the world today. In fact, there was very little area of the human landscape not visited by the exploring imagination of Shakespeare and the dialectical intellect of Donne. And they were (as poets often are) unusually more sensitive to their environments than their more 'fortunate' contemporaries in the circle of society that mattered were, with the result that they reacted in ways dictated by their individual temperaments. Shakespeare, not necessarily owing to a philosophical bent of mind, possessed the peculiar ability of emotional detachment necessary for an objective assessment of life—a phenomenon Keats has found convenient to call 'Negative Capability':

> That is, when man is capable of being in uncertainties, mysteries, doubts, without any irritable reaching after fact & reason.[1]

For there is more to life than what any man can take for granted, understand or even believe is possible. This may be the reason why tragedy loses much of its excess in Shakespeare. "A strong faith tends to render tragedy impossible" says G. Wilson Knight.[2] To a man whose knowledge of life lends him the capability to accept life in all its aspects, the agony and the ecstasy, faith comes naturally: faith in human nature, faith in the future, faith in evil—provided that man 'distils it out'. The singularity of Shakespeare as a dramatist is that even the darkest of his tragedies end in optimistic expectancy of a regenerated society after the ideal catharses have taken effect.

Where does this universal empathy in Shakespeare derive from? It was perhaps Dryden who first answered this question, when in his famous encomium, he attributes to him "the largest and the most comprehensive soul" which, by implication, assumes the nature of a microcosm of humanity. If it is true that our opinions of others and the world at large are modified projections of our egos, we may not have to seek farther than Shakespeare's own heart for the fountain of this universal goodwill and understanding. In that case, it would make little difference were the Beauteous Friend of the Sonnets more responsive to the Poet's pleadings than being "too much in love with himself to get married and be bound to a particular woman."[3]

In the case of Donne too, undone as he was for loving too well, it has been a fond conceit with him to place himself in his mistress's heart and eyes as a way of perfecting the desired union. Or sometimes, the union is sanguinarily achieved inside the body of the flea which has bitten him and later his mistress. And drops of farewell tears bearing their images dissolve into each other symbolically.

The nature of *love* in the works of Shakespeare and Donne is of the kind familiar to all men and women, ranging from the primary instinct of procreation to a higher and nobler attribute conducive to social harmony. While the main action takes place in terms of normal relationship between man and woman, which has more or less been the limit of courtly love, the lovers in the works of Shakespeare and Donne are more ambitious of reaching a higher plane of happiness than what physical consummation of love can afford. Ironically, love pursued for the sake of the senses tends to destroy the very end of it: the satisfaction of total union.

> Enjoy'd no sooner but despised straight.
>
> *(Sonnet 129)*

For it is realized, perhaps sooner than desired, that after all, lovers' union is of a higher order than physical experience, the highest moment of which slips through the fingers like a dream. When you think you have it, then it is gone; but the memory of it lingers, and the lovers can never be again what they were before the loss of innocence, their love-making having left.

> A kinde of sorrowing dulnesse to the minde.[4]

Shakespeare too could hardly have uttered a stronger condemnation of this Ovidian *amore di amore* than he did in Sonnet 129:

> A bliss in proof, and prov'd, a very woe;
> Before, a joy propos'd, behind a dream.

Perhaps, one should not be blamed for saying that English Love Poetry reached its full maturity with Shakespeare and Donne. Sir Herbert Read appears to have no qualms in stating that, "There is no aspect of love that is not covered by Shakespeare's poetry",[5] and concurring with Grierson that:

> It is only in the fragments of Sapho, the lyrics of Catullus, and the songs of Burns that one will find the sheer joy of loving and being loved expressed in the same direct and simple language as in some of Donne's songs, only Browning that one will find the same simplicity of feeling combined with a like swift and subtle dialectic.[6]

Love has come a long way from rustic courtship to its stylized conventionalization as courtly love, and thence to its liberation from the insidious dichotomy of institutionalization.

More than ever in the past,—perhaps owing to the sharpening awareness of fresh promises of life opened up by the Renaissance humanism—the consciousness of temporality in poetry became increasingly acute and pervasive in the Elizabethan age. Sickness and wars aggravated fears of impending death. Religious pietism, instead of providing peace and security, encouraged constant fear of impending doom as a means to keep men virtuous. Medieval scholasticism had viewed pleasure, either of thought or of the senses, with suspicion, denouncing even the pursuit of earthly love. The transience of earthly joys in contrast to the permanence of the love of Christ had become conventional in poetry for almost four hundred years.[7]

> Love only love, and hate the filth of sin;
> Give Christ your soul, that we [sic] may dwell within;
> For as he bought it, sought it, seeks it, so
> Shall you have bliss, and heaven in you grow.
>
> The nature of love is this: where it is true,
> It stays forever and will not change for new.
> Who holds, or once possessed, love in his mind,
> Is saved from care, and heart's delight shall find.
> ... ...
> But fleshly love is like a flower in May,
> And scarcely lasts an hour in the day:
> And then desire and joy and pride lament
> In lasting woe their sad predicament.[8]

A contrary reaction to the cramped feeling of being Time's prey appeared in such popular literary motif as *carpe diem* appearing in Herrick's 'To the Virgins, To Make Much of Time' (*Gather ye rosebuds while ye may*), Spenser's 'Faerie Queene' (*Gather therefore the Rose, whilest yet is prime*— II.xxi. 74), Marvell's 'To His Coy Mistress' (*Now therefore, while the youthful hue Sits on thy skin...*)

It will be seen in the following chapter how the majority of Medieval poems treat of love within a religious framework, clothing it with the ideal of courtly love. This apparent dearth of secular love poems need not be taken to mean that medieval life was exceptionally pious and chaste. The few surviving secular love-poems such as the *MS Harley 2253* as well as the works of Chaucer and Spenser testify to the sensuousness of the age.

Another interesting explanation has been made by John Speirs in his valuable study of Medieval English Poetry:

> ...a large proportion of medieval lyrics owe their preservation to having been copied and kept in religious houses. The ecclesiastical authorities, upon whom the preservation in MS must largely have depended up to the end of the fourteenth century, would not have been particularly concerned to preserve profane songs—unless these had been first sanctified, transformed into Christian songs. That may be the reason why so many Christian religious lyrics have been preserved. There is little doubt that the medieval communities as a whole were more pagan than appears from the written evidence. It is clear from these records [i.e., of ecclesiastical denunciations and prohibitions which indicate active opposition on the part of the Church to profane songs and dance] alone that profane song was associated with old Paganism, its rites and dances.[9]

One such poem echoes the nineteenth Elegy of Donne:

> A pleasing mouth to frame her thought,
> Lips red and true, expressly wrought
> A fine romance to read.
> As sweetly set as any known,
> Her teeth are white as whale-bone;
> Let courtly men take heed.
> Her swan-like neck is truly set,
> And longer than I ever met,
> A perfect pleasure indeed!
> I'd rather wait for her to come
> Than be the Pope and ride in Rome
> In pomp upon a steed.

The catalogue of sensuous body fills three more stanzas, concluding in a sanctimonious inducement to possess the same as a gift from God:

> A man were blest in Jesu's sight
> If he could lie with her at night,
> For he'd have heaven here.[10]

For all its ascetic idealism the "great theocratic age of England"[11] could not suppress the vitality of its amatory element. Indeed, a closer inspection of the courtly ideal of love reveals gross contradictions between that ideal of chastity in poetry and its application to life often slyly hinted. With the virtuous lady, the inspirer of courtly love, often proving to be another man's wife, and the significant rejection of marital institution as the proper end of love, the halo of courtly romance appears to be no more than a camouflage for the pursuit of love beyond the marital dimension wherein love justifies its devotees. The liberating effect on the mind of the Renaissance had perhaps been contributory to the unmasking of courtly love, working hand in hand with the scepticism following new scientific discoveries. The fear of judgement of sinners that had been the strongest rallying weapon of the Church began to lose its menace when

> New Philosophy calls all in doubt,
> The element of fire is quite put out;
> The sun is lost, and th'earth, and no man's wit
> Can well direct him where to looke for it.
>
> *(The First Anniversary)*

This relief from the oppressive weight of religious intolerance of worldly values, while giving rein to man's sensual nature, also created an uncomfortable void where there had been a definite purpose for and a meaning to a life of virtue. The recession of heavenly Paradise opened the moral universe to the usurpation of Time. The stability of faith in eternal life was replaced by an uneasy feeling of insecurity, and a pervasive powerful awareness of mortality and impermanence. Hence, the strong and insistent cry to assert life and make the most of it. The hope of eternal happiness was exchanged for a more tangible, but ephemeral, happiness subject to an unpredictable law of mutability—by which is known the ineluctable, and highly unstable motion of a blind impersonal universe ticking away unconscionably like a clock in a ball-room.

Mutability may be stated as the law or system which explains the changes in nature and the instability of order in the universe, both of which are attendant upon the continuous movement of time. In its essence, which is constant interchange of states, mutability is the reverse of eternity. Even when time and mutability are felt to be inescapable, they are recognized as preludes to eternity of which they are the moving image. To the medieval mind not yet troubled by the Renaissance attitude of rationalism, the concept of time and mutability posed less of a threat to man's will to life and immortality than as a warning of their effect upon the brief span of life allotted to man, and as an exhortation to make use of time in preparing for eternity. But as the concept of eternity grew more diffused towards the Renaissance, the attitude to time and mutability also grew more alarmed and depressing.

While it is undoubtedly the work of the Renaissance to usher in the Scepticism which began to undermine the received faith, we may also see in the new spirit of 'humanism', a strong insistence on justifying the moral aspects of the Renaissance. For the humanism of the early Renaissance, unlike its later development, honestly believed in giving emphasis on the practical aspect of Christian values. They believed that

> man's existence, far from being a brief and painful preparation for the afterlife, could, through exercise of human reason and talents, offer fulfillment in life.[12]

However, the strain of trying to bridge the two worlds—the world of unconditional faith and the world of examined faith—was severe, as strikingly portrayed by Marlowe in *Dr Faustus*. And it is difficult to determine how far the Renaissance humanism succeeded in resolving the casuistical questions attending on this transition.

Shakespeare's plays afford significant explorations into the mind of Renaissance man. They reveal the limits of human faculties against the vast and unfathomable backdrop of unknown universe. Renaissance man is pitted against his own ignorance on this arena called 'space-time', with the spectators —assuming there are—sitting behind one-way glass partition, having little or no communication with the contestants. Time and mutability have never been treated merely as philosophical concepts by the Renaissance writers. They are seen and treated as moral forces bearing significantly on human actions. The voice of Marcus Aurelius still echoes down the ages through his writings which are now assimilated assiduously like living waters:

> Therefore make your passage through this span of time in obedience to Nature and gladly lay down your life, as an olive, when ripe, might fall, blessing her who bear it and grateful to the tree which gave it life.[13]

This is not too far from the stoicism of an Edgar or a Gloucester. T.S. Eliot has expressed his view that the Elizabethan age had a certain affinity to the brutal age of the Roman empire when

> Stoicism is the refuge for the individual in an indifferent or hostile world too big for him.[14]

Once the long respected guardian of man's thoughts—the Church—has been found inadequate to answer man's curiosity, and man begins to search the inner recesses of his own mind for an explanation of the riddle of life, it is only inevitable that pessimism should set in where man discovers his limitations. Contrary to popular views of the Renaissance as an enlightened age of optimism, Sukanta Chaudhuri observes ominously:

> More and more evidence may be gathered to suggest that the Renaissance was not simply a glorious 'rebirth' but an age of collapsing values and systems, of disturbance, exhaustion, and deep humility.[15]

It is no wonder, therefore, that we find a proliferation of love poetry during the Renaissance. For once, the wonted solace of faith in the spiritual and the intangible aspect of human experience has lost its credit, what is left of any possible cause for the will to life having any stamp of honour is only love—the only transcending virtue capable of giving consolation. Love, as in medieval time, is still inspired by beauty. But it is no more an idealized pursuit of chastity and heroism as an overture to spiritual bliss. The object and inspirer of love, the beautiful woman, deconventionalized, becomes a woman of flesh and blood, to possess whom is the ideal of the lover. In place of the knight-errant in perpetual quest to prove his physical prowess and moral impeccability, we have the lover-courtier snobbishly cramming up philosophy and with crumpled love poems in his pocket, sighing like a furnace.

The medieval ethics of love apparently showed its intrinsic weakness in that it failed utterly to accommodate sex for reasons too obvious to mention. The medieval dichotomy successfully suppressed the carnal aspect of love so long as religion and illiteracy held back the free and individual expression that the Renaissance was to foster. But we see in the works of Chaucer how the spirit of love has been yearning for release, and vigorously stating its case in the person of the Wife of Bath, as well as in the Franklin's and the Merchant's tales. In Spenser, that great interpreter of Medieval ethics for the Renaissance, "The medieval dichotomy is being bridged"[16], the taboo smashed and exposed for what it really is, while virtue and chastity become 'earthly' ideals. For Spenser makes of love "a perfectly satisfying spiritual experience without transcending its human, erotic character. Sacred and profane love meet in Spenser's chastity."[17] But the strain was hard on the potential of man: the ideal of an 'earthly' purity seemed no easier than the attainment of a 'spiritual' renunciatory ideal of sainthood.

It is in Donne that we find a more successful synthesis of the hitherto incompatible ideals. This he has done by a more 'scientific' temperament capable of taking for granted the 'imperfections' of the human condition as the ground in which love must take root. If at all a transcendence of any kind is expected of Donne, it will be in the moral attitude to sexual love which J.B. Leishman prefers to call "religiousness"[18] so strikingly paramount in his love poetry. But the fusion Donne seems to have achieved in his love poems, like the very conceits which convey them, appears but as a shooting star; real but ephemeral. While Donne's poetry treats of love in all its aspects —from sterile Platonic love to love that kills "with excess of heat"—there is ample evidence to show that Donne was writing (and living) under severe constraints and conflicts. The conflicts are, however, not so much between what C.S. Lewis calls "a medieval sense of the sinfulness of sexuality"[19] and unabashed celebration of "Gentle love deeds", as they are between the inner (timeless) experience of love and the external (temporal) experience of love which are mutually complementary to and interdependent on each other for a full experience of love, while mutually tending to cancel each other. The strong insistence of *The Extasie* that there is "Small change, when we're to bodies gone" is after all conditioned by a stronger "If" that their

> two loves be one, or, thou and I
> Love so alike, that none doe slacken, none can die.

This apprehension attending on the highest moment of love is characteristic of Donne who, like any sensitive man of his time, could not afford to turn a deaf ear to the call of time. In fact, the very insistence on the totality of the lovers' experience can be seen as a direct challenge to Time and Mutability. And this is the most typical and most persistent voice of Elizabethan and Jacobean love poets. However, hardly any poet of the time stands comparison with Shakespeare and Donne in the depth and range of the treatment of human love in the context of temporality and an unstable order. While the majority of their contemporaries instinctively recoiled at the cold touch of reality, advocating an Epicurean attitude to life to spite the horrors of tomorrow, Shakespeare and Donne showed quite a different attitude to the grim reality of Time's supremacy over human achievement. Theirs is a more lasting vindication of love in a world they dramatize as intrinsically hostile to it. And this they have done by a higher and nobler sense of man's worth and faith in man's indomitable spirit to subordinate his situation in life. More than in the works of any of their contemporaries, we are presented in their works with the nearest approximation in imaginative form to the Renaissance picture of man. What is of paramount importance in Donne's final rejection of love, therefore, is his sense of the failure of love to sustain the moment of perfect unity, and not the moral problem of sexuality which Donne has transcended in the purity of his concept of love.

It has become customary to call Shakespeare's love for the 'Beauteous youth' of the Sonnets platonic in a gross misunderstanding of the term. The Platonic concept of love as "desire for the perpetual possession of the good", and whose object is not beauty but "to procreate and bring forth in beauty"[20], more truly applies to Shakespeare's idea of love for a friend than it defines the nature of relationship between them. But what should rather concern the reader of the Sonnets is the almost paranoiac obsession with the effect of time on the Friend's beauty and the instability of man's estate which deprives man of what little joy and happiness he finds in his brief allotted time. Just as Donne puts himself in his mistress's heart and eyes, Shakespeare, embodied in his love, lives or dies in the beauty of his Friend. Hence, the urgency of his cry to make war on Time by procreation.

> Make thee another self, for love of me,
> That beauty still may live in thine or thee.

(Sonnet 10)

For Beauty is the real 'food of love' while it is much the prey to Time. Beauty and love are doomed:

> All lovers young, all lovers must
> Consign to thee and come to dust.

(Cymbeline, 4.2.275)

So overpowering is this knowledge that Shakespeare gives it a universal apocalyptic scale in *Sonnet 64*, and again in *The Tempest* (4.1.151-58). Man, the pride of Creation, is seen in his true dimension in the scale of the Universe. Donne's vision of this diminution of Man in *The First Anniversary* is a morally degenerate being in the process of self-annihilation trying to out-god God:

> Wee seeme ambitious, Gods whole worke t'undoe;
> Of nothing hee made us, and we strive too,
> To bring our selves to nothing backe. (155-57)

The graveyard scene in *Hamlet*, more than the prince's famous declamatory speech on man and the cosmos, shows the nadir of Shakespeare's naturalistic world view. It is some conjecture to think what Shakespeare might have written had he looked at this beautiful blue ball from out in space like Armstrong!

Imperious Caesar, dead and turn'd to clay,
Might stop a hole to keep the wind away.
O, that that earth which kept the world in awe
Should patch a wall t'expel the winter's flaw!

(5.1.207-10)

What a thought! Would not Tennyson have written this with Hamlet in his mind as well as Hallam:

And he, shall he,
... ...
Who loved, who suffered countless ills,
Who battled for the True, the Just,
Be blown about the desert dust,
Or sealed within the iron hills?
... ...
What hope of answer, or redress?
Behind the veil, behind the veil. *(In Memoriam, 61)*

What is the end of man, and what is the purpose of his life, are recurrent questions the "unquiet heart and brain"[21] of man ask through the ages; no less Shakespeare's. And for the Renaissance humanist, it is especially significant as the growing feathers of man's aspiration need the special glue that will not melt in the hot sun of his own rationalism. It is significant that there are no Providential interventions in Shakespeare's plays by way of grace or retribution apart from the working out of Time in the irreversible law of mutability, wherein

... the whirligig of time brings in his revenges[22]

and rewards. Shakespeare's universe is self-sustaining, where every action is stored up in a retrieval system, and nothing comes of nothing. Even the island magic of Prospero is tolerated as a dramatic license which can never be admitted in Milan. Whenever Shakespeare needs to bring in an element of strangeness, it must be in the by-ways and suburbs of normal society—the woods outside Athens, the forest of Arden, a dark guard platform, the wild heath, and superstitious minds.

The macabre figure of faceless Death with a long scythe overlooked the landscape of Shakespeare's world like a monument of oblivion. Keats wrote his poem, *Bright Star*, on a blank page in his copy of Shakespeare's Poems, clinging passionately to life and promised love—his only reality:

> Bright star, would I were stedfast as thou art—
> Not in lone splendour hung aloft the night
> ... ...
> No—yet still stedfast, still unchangeable,
> Pillowed upon my fair love's ripening breast,
> To feel forever its soft fall and swell,
> Awake forever in a sweet unrest ....
> And so live ever—or else swoon to death.

The same tragic irony of an elusive, unrealized happiness recurs again and again in Shakespeare as a result of Time's fickleness, as in *Romeo and Juliet*. But the tragedy of loss that Keats feels often loses its sting in Shakespeare when lovers simply refuse to let Time undo their love. Antony and Cleopatra find in death the true union of souls neither empires nor sex can give. Just as Macbeth tried to abbreviate time to serve his ambition, the lovers in *Romeo and Juliet* make a drudge of Time as they do the Nurse; and in a manner which calls on Time's revenge.[23] The irreligiousness of Romeo, so typical of a teenage lover, can hardly be paralleled in its hubristic recklessness:

> *Friar L.* So smile the heavens upon this holy act
> That after-hours with sorrow chide us not!
>
> *Romeo.* Amen, amen! But come what sorrow can,
> It cannot countervail the exchange of joy
> That one short minute gives me in her sight.
> Do thou but close our hands with holy words,
> Then love-devouring death do what he dare;
> It is enough I may but call her mine.

Calling forth a grim prognosis from the Friar:

> These violent delights have violent ends,
> And in their triumph die; like fire and powder,
> Which, as thy kiss, consume. The sweet honey
> Is loathsome in his own deliciousness,
> And in the taste confounds the appetite.
> Therefore love moderately: long love doth so;
> Too swift arrives as tardy as too slow. (2.6.1-15)

The tragedy of love that often derives from deprivation of lovers' earthly happiness, while assuming the physical consummation of love as the chief reward of love, holds out in clear perspective the truth that love is not fulfilled in sensual terms. Shakespeare leaves no doubt about his attitude to love informed by the senses; neither does he equate sex with love as essential complements. Juliet is indeed a little 'hot' as her Nurse says, to whom love is no more than being hot. And Romeo hardly thinks of the marriage ceremony more than as a means to 'call her mine'. But neither marriage vows nor bridal night yields lasting happiness. The ultimate test of love comes when the lover has to choose between his love and his life. Those who accuse Cleopatra of being a strumpet find their rebuff at seeing her choose death rather than live another strumpet life. Juliet still has an opportunity to live a new life, even if we consider the same chance for Romeo a little too slim. Valentine exhibits true love in willing to lose Sylvia's hand to Proteus if only to show what love is; and Bassanio parts with his wife's gift on Antonio's request, to be forgiven for the love which prompted him. Tragedy comes when the fruit is mistaken for the tree that bears it. The lovers' fantasy of permanence is not to be found in the continual flux of time and mutability, but is a reality lovers experience in the timeless consciousness of their need for each other.

Shakespeare's essential humanism reveals itself in the ambiguity of his tragic catharsis. By this is meant, the tenacious optimism of Shakespeare, his inexorable faith in the human will to override his fate, by which tragedy is often robbed of its sting, and a perfect catharsis, all the more desirable for the welcome way in which even death is met, is achieved. Not only the death of a Hamlet, a Lear, or an Othello, but that of a Richard II, a Richard III, or a Macbeth is relieved by shows of indomitable will to trample on their fates.

And yet, the greatest significance of Shakespeare to the modern world may be for the fresh hope he has brought to life by resolving the claims of Love and Time in his later Comedies. The mature Shakespeare is a man who has come to realize the irresistible forces man has to contend with. Man is not a beast whose "chief good and market of his time" is "but to sleep and feed". Man differs from beast less in anatomy than in what he does with his anatomy. To quote J. Bronowski, a noted biologist,

> Among the multitude of animals which scamper, fly, burrow and swim around us, man is the only one who is not locked into his environment. His imagination, his reason, his emotional subtlety and toughness, make it possible for him not to accept the environment but to change it.[24]

Time and his own mortality are environments which man can never modify to suit himself, but he may modify his attitude to them so as to relieve his sense of fate. The Senecan stoicism of an Edgar robs life of the glory of the strife. It is the voice of a world whose 'inhabitants' see themselves as victims, a world wherein

> Humanity must perforce prey on itself.
>
> (Lear 4.2.48)

The world hardly changes in the later Romances. The storms still rage; the bear bites; tempers run high still; pride, jealousy, lust and ambition prevail. But the lovers here possess a certain miraculous power to withstand all kinds of adverse circumstances, and to evolve into new creatures that can turn adversity to advantage. Duke Senior learns his lesson in a much more pleasant way than King Lear. Leontes and Pericles take their fates much like Gloucester, till love awakens them from their tragic brooding. Portia gains a true lover by a means which could possibly deprive her of her only love. Viola's suit becomes her blessing through her efforts to bless another.

Love in Shakespeare finally becomes a moral force which brings together in its warm embrace, not only man and woman for propagation, but all who have learnt to swim along the stream of events. One reason why Shakespeare does not treat love in the 'carpe diem' spirit is perhaps due to his unerring faith in life wherein 'the whirligig of time' brings in not only his revenges, but rewards too. Once love is born, Prospero is prepared to renounce his magic to face the world inhabited by the Antonios and the Sebastians, whose repentance hardly convince us. It is Leontes's undying love for Hermione that brings her back to him. Yet this might never have happened but for the love between Florizel and Perdita. It is Love that shows

> How far that little candle throws his beams

to Portia, who has just done a good deed of love that shines like the candle in the 'naughty' world infested with the likes of Shylock.

This treatment of love as virtually the prime motivating spirit of harmony in society is a new thing in literature, which medieval Christianity had failed to discover. This spirit of love capable of so much self-sacrifice and tolerance, this spirit of love which "bears it out even to the edge of doom", and does not "bends with the remover to remove", is a truer gospel than what medieval Christendom had preached. By weaving the delicate and fragile thread of love through the labyrinthine maze of life, Shakespeare (and Donne too in a more limited sense) seems to point out that it is only love that can resolve the problems with which mankind finds itself hemmed in on all sides. The consequence of mishandling this vital link with life is stated unreservedly by both Shakespeare and Donne, showing us the rotten feeling left by love when lust is served. Love to them is a motion of the entire personality, surging forth from the inmost depth of the soul, and not a mere physical appetite that can be surfeited with sensory experience. This is what Enobarbus sees in Cleopatra's enigmatic love:

> Her passions are made of nothing but the finest part of pure love.... This cannot be cunning in her.
>
> *(Ant & Cleo.* 1.2.142)

Character, not beauty—the 'loveliness within', to use Donne's expression—is the base on which Shakespeare and Donne, in the final analysis, erect their image of love. The choice of caskets in *The Merchant of Venice*, the constancy of Desdemona, Hermione, Marina, defenceless even in innocence; the incorruptible optimism of Portia, Viola and Rosalind; the resoluteness and bravery of Cordelia and Imogen, are all alike indicative of this.

Time usually assumes something of the role of a character in Shakespeare's works. It conditions the poet's sensibilities concerning love and human dignity. It is the poet's acute sense of Time's supremacy over the entire creation to which we must attribute his constant assertion of the power of love over that of Time:

> Love's not Time's fool, though rosy lips and cheeks
> Within his bending sickle's compass come;
> Love alters not with his brief hours and weeks,
> But bears it out even to the edge of doom.
>
> (*Sonnet* 116)

This is not a defeat of Time but a victory over Time's power on transience and mortality. Put this alongside Donne's poems on the same topic, like *The Anniversarie, The Good-morrow, Love's Growth, Death be not Proud*, and we have a symphony of kindred spirit singing in unison the true and noble aspiration of the human soul striving against his 'mortal coil'. Time in Donne's poetry does not so much impress mortality and 'beauty's doom', as it spells out the period of love in contradistinction to the atemporal nature of lovers' experience. For Donne is concerned in his love poetry with the precise nature of the full experience of love, taking into account the full-blooded sensory experience as well as the emotional experience of total unity.

> All other things, to their destruction draw,
> Only our love hath no decay;
> This, no tomorrow hath, nor yesterday,
> Running it never runs from us away,
> But truly keeps his first, last, everlasting day.
>
> *(The Anniversarie)*

Yet, notwithstanding Donne's assertion that there is

> Small change, when we're to bodies gone,
>
> (*The Ecstasie*)

and that,

> Love must not be, but take a body too,
>
> (*Aire and Angels*)

It is obvious that by relying on the body which is subject to time, love has become subject to time and the law of mutability. Love is then measured by the unit of time:

> For I had rather owner bee
> Of thee one houre, then all else ever. (*A Feaver*)

The disquieting presence of Time as an invigilator in the person of the prying sun may be 'eclipsed' with a 'wink' of self-deception; but the very action of denying time's reality has also become a denial of love's reality:

> Me thinkes I lyed all winter, when I swore
> My love was infinite, if spring make it more.
>
> (*Love's growth*)

> Love is a growing, or full constant light;
> And his first minute, after noone, is night.
>
> (*A Lecture upon the Shadow*)

Love must be rejected, therefore, if it proves to be illusory heaven, if it is "onely for a minute made to be". (*Farewell to Love*). It is this conflict between the 'stasis' (still time) of lovers' experience and the irresistible movement of time which punctuates love's eternity that lends all the force, the urgency and the pathos of Donne's poetry.

Thus we find Donne sharing with Shakespeare the overwhelming consciousness of Time's challenge to the human will to gain a hold on eternity. The passion and the pathos of his poems derive from the intensity of his desire to transubstantiate the moment of love's perfection. Perhaps Donne has found the best medium at his disposal, as Shakespeare does, in his poetry.

NOTES

1. Letter to George and Tom Keats, December 21, 27(?), 1817, *Oxford Anthology of English Literature*, ed. Frank Kermode, et al., 1973, p. 768.
2. *The Crown of Life*, Methuen, 1982, p. 35.
3. S.C. Sen Gupta, *A Shakespeare Manual*, OUP (Cal), 1982, p. 177
4. Donne, *Farewell to Love*, All quotations of Donne's poems are from H.J.C. Grierson's edition, *Donne: Poetical Works*, OUP, 1977.
5. *Phases of English Poetry*, Greenwood, USA, 1972, p. 67.
6. *Ibid.*, p. 75.
7. Brian Stone, *Medieval English Verse*, Penguin, 1964, pp. 14-15.
8. *Ibid.*, p. 58, *Poems of Adoration No. 23.*
9. *Medieval English Poetry: The Non-Chaucerian Tradition*, Faber & Faber, 1971, p. 46.
10. Brian Stone, *op. cit.*, pp. 203-04.
11. Frederick Turner, *Shakespeare and the Nature of Time*, Oxford, 1971, p. 180.
12. Karl Beckson and Arthur Ganz, *Literary Terms, a Dictionary*, Rupa & Co. (India), 1971, p. 228.
13. *Meditations of Marcus Aurelius Antoninus*, tr. & ed. A.S. Farquharson, 1944; as quoted in F. Turner, *op. cit.*, p. 178.
14. 'Shakespeare and the Stoicism of Seneca', in *Selected Essays*, (1927), p. 132.
15. *Infirm Glory: Shakespeare and the Renaissance Image of Man*, Clarendon (Oxford), 1981, p. 2.
16. *Ibid.*, p. 88.
17. *Ibid.*, p. 92.
18. *Themes and Variations in Shakespeare's Sonnets*, London, 1961, p. 218.
19. 'Donne and Love Poetry in the Seventeenth Century', *John Donne: Twentieth Century Views Series*, ed. Helen Gardner, Prentice-Hall, India, 1962, p. 90.
20. Plato, *The Symposium*, tr. W. Hamilton, Penguin, Hammondsworth, 1951, pp. 86-87.
21. Tennyson, *In Memoriam*, VI.
22. Christopher Marlowe, *Edward II.*
23. John Lawlor, *Romeo and Juliet*, 'Stratford-upon-Avon Studies: 3 Early Shakespeare', ed. John Russell, et al., Arnold, 1971, p. 127.
24. *The Ascent of Man*, Futura, 1981, p. 14.

2

Love in Medieval and Early Renaissance English Poetry

We've made a great mess of love
Since we made an ideal of it.

D.H. Lawrence—'The Mess of Love'

Love, as modern man has come to understand it, could well be the discovery of the Middle ages. And its emergence in the form of 'courtly love' is indicative of the specific nature of its pursuit, which more or less required freedom from tillage and a fine sensibility. Love, as such was, therefore, "essentially an aristocratic experience".[1] Since classical literature and society treated love only at the "levels of merry sensuality or domestic comfort",[2]—evidence of classic honesty and courage possessed by the heathen world—it is only to be expected that medieval Christendom should develop a purple patch where it failed to realize its moral ideals.

> The failure to incorporate love into the purpose of marital intercourse was largely a failure of theological analysis.[3]

This is not surprising in view of the orthodox teaching on the sacrament of Christian marriage which makes no allowance for passionate love other than for procreation and prevention of adultery—still in force. The employment of sex in marriage has been, then and now, a duty and a biological function: a totally degrading experience from the viewpoint of courtly love.

In Medieval Christian marriage, love had no relevance. Marriage was an economic and political transaction, either to improve living condition or to acquire power or both. The woman might have been an ideal beauty inspiring heroic exploits and deserving loyal service; but once married, she became a mere possession of her husband, losing any economic rights and ownership she had enjoyed before marriage.[4] Love between spouses in such cultural context was not just meaningless, but a contradiction. C.S. Lewis is neither exaggerating nor being cynical when saying,

> Any idealization of sexual love, in a society where marriage is purely utilitarian, must begin by being an idealization of adultery.[5]

And since love affair with a virgin has marriage as its ideal consummation, the passionate intensity that courtly love required invariably derived from an affair with a married woman. If the context of courtly love were understood sufficiently, the love of Lancelot and Guinevere needs not be shocking as it is apt to be so by modern standards.

We need not, however, see the ennoblement of lust as an inevitable alternative to marriage in quest of a higher fulfillment. The subject of poetry has always been the high passions that move men and women to actions which make or mar their destiny. The placid and resigned mood fostered by marriage hardly ever inspires poetry. It is when his hopes and aspirations, his desires and expectations are being threatened or destroyed that man stands in his full stature, when the mysteries of the depths of his personality emerge on the surface in living poetry. An unquiet marriage, unapproved love, over-protected young girls, social and economic disparity between lovers: these are some of the most frequently exploited themes. The rise of feudalism, with its castles and rich *beau monde*, provided a highly suitable world of romance. The very closeness of castle life—where sexes and classes mixed in a bee-hive communal harmony running on an elaborate system of etiquette—made it an ideal breeding ground for varieties of love under the umbrella of courtly love.

Of the conventional aspects of courtly love, just a few words of generalization are needed to refresh one's memory. Its native home was southern France, and it flourished during the twelfth and thirteenth centuries as the works of the troubadours. Very few things are as neatly dove-tailed as are the structure of feudalism and the manner of courtly love. Here woman, very often the lady of the castle, becomes the ideal of feminine virtue deserving love and service of the man who must prove his sincerity by physical and moral courage. In an age when dangers and adventures were considered the essential ingredients of the manly virtue of chivalry, the dangers of courtly love (infrequently coming from a jealous husband while others were ignorant of being cuckolded) provided all the better atmosphere of a romantic adventure. The more the danger, the more intense the experience and deeper the commitment of the lovers.

The popularity of courtly love celebrated by the troubadours in Provence became universal in the western Europe with the works of Chretien de Troyes, whose famous romances, *Lancelot, Yvain* and *Perceval* greatly influenced Chaucer and Malory. The Arthurian legends had long been popular in France even before Geoffrey of Monmouth (d. 1154) gave them historical authenticity with his *Historia Regum Britanniae.* But it seems that it was the psychological analysis of love in the Ovidian style that Chretien made which helped to establish the chivalric code of love in the life and literature of medieval Europe. While Ovid incurred royal displeasure by the effects his *Ars Amatoria* allegedly had on young ladies, Chretien showed more discretion by tempering his love with the love of virtue.[6] In an age when sharp social difference narrowed the world of *fine amour*, and sensual love beyond that was seen as adultery or prostitution, courtly romance needed to weave moral precepts into its sensual patterns by allegorizing the stories of love and heroism. Hence, it is a matter of subjective questioning whether the study of these romances as moral allegory is more profitable than to see the moral allegory as a means to expose vice and hypocrisy in high society.

What Dante did to his Italy, Geoffrey Chaucer (1340-1400) has done to England, i.e., expose courtly love for what it really is; but in a merrier manner than his more spiritually inclined counterpart. England, however, cannot be compared with Italy, or with France. The colder climate and the more serious temperament of the people of England tended to moderate the spirit of courtly love as suggested by the stress given on the moral aspects of the romances which came there mostly by translations.

Whatever native literature England produced at this time had been fairly religious. A gloomy sense of earthly transience and vulnerability of human existence had already set in, expressed in the elegiac tone of the didactic poems of the Anglo-Saxon period. And well into the Norman period till the coming of Chaucer, the prevailing note had been one of ascetic idealism, the imported romances receiving a colder reception than they might have enjoyed in the south. For the more secular and sophisticated courtly sentiment of the French original was as a rule, left out by the English translators in favour of the adventure story which the cruder English sentiment could appreciate.[7]

By bringing in the lighter vein of French poetry into his native literature, Chaucer prefigures the Renaissance in England. There had already flourished in France, a new kind of literature called the 'Fabliau',

> a type of short narrative poem, realistic, humorous, often coarse...associated with the new middle classes who slowly grew in importance as the feudal system developed only to decay.[8]

These fabliaux reflected the attitude of the new gentry towards the idle pastimes of the leisured landlords who lived and laughed and played at the expense of serfs. They were

> less impressed by the courtly notions of love and honor than the more conservative feudal landowners; realistic, iconoclastic, priding themselves on knowing life as it really is and on refusing to look at it through the rose-coloured spectacles of sentimental idealists.[9]

The "boisterous, satirical kind of narrative...the antitype of the idealizing vision of courtly knight or pious churchman"[10] fitted the self-reliant temper of the new bourgeoisie whose self-made world could not afford to lose sight of reality. The debt of Chaucer to the fabliaux is apparent in the tales of the Canterbury pilgrims. But it is the spirit in which Chaucer introduced these tales of cuckoldry and vices which draws our attention.

The allegorical mode had already been sufficiently developed to become the medium of courtly romance as a result of Christianity which encouraged or even necessitated the objectification of mental and spiritual conditions,[11] when Chaucer translated *Roman de la Rose*. This work, which is the most elaborate specimen of allegorical romance of the Middle Ages, is the work of two men. The first part was composed by Guillaume de Lorris about 1227 AD, and the second by Jean de Meun between 1268-77. Lorris's part of the book, some twenty-two thousand lines, is in the tradition of the true allegory of courtly love: the 'rose' representing the lady's love enclosed within a garden hedge.

> The whole background of the story is courtly life, a life of leisure and good breeding, where there is nothing to do but dance and sing and make love.[12]

Taking up Lorris's unfinished work about forty years later, Meun introduced a totally different spirit into his work. In place of the magical dream-like world of ideal love, we find a mocking realism which is characteristic of the new skeptical bourgeoisie. "Meun is still working within the courtly tradition, but he is out of sympathy with it."[13]

The development of Chaucer's art and philosophy of love from almost youthful effervescence with the joy of life to the almost detached satirical humour and skepticism of maturity has been traced by most historians and critics in relation to the metamorphosis of his works, as well as through his continual attachment to individual works such as the *Roman de la Rose.*[14]

This work proved to be a double inspiration to him: in his youth by its graceful love-allegory, and in his manhood by its mature realism. As a young man of good favour, and later of great experience as soldier, diplomat and official, Chaucer's observation of real life in the higher circles should naturally have resulted in a cynical rejection of its values. That Chaucer retained his faith in love and in life is a great credit to his instinctive love of mankind whose faults and foibles may be corrected by clear vision of the truth of life.

But the real fame of Chaucer rests on two works of his so-named Italian Period and English Period—*Troilus and Criseyde* (1372-84) and *The Canterbury Tales* (1387-1400).

Love in war-torn Ilium motivated Shakespeare's genius to study the nature of love under extreme circumstances, showing how love relates to man in society. The same event provided Chaucer with an opportunity to examine the nature of courtly love, and strip it naked to reveal its essential fleshliness. To do this, Chaucer did not have to develop the character of Troilus beyond the conventional cast of a courtly lover, whose ultimate achievement was embodied in the possession of Criseyde as a lover. It is in the character of Criseyde and her rationalization of love that Chaucer achieved the first psychological study of a woman's mind. She is a prefigurement of the Shakespearean heroine in her self-possessed, witty, modest and circumspect nature, ready to face life on her own. Lu Emily Pearson feelingly analyses her actions, attributing them to those very female virtues which make her endearing:

> The author's account of the seduction of Criseyde perfectly reconciles the weakness of human nature with the code. Criseyde believed her uncle's story of the mad jealousy of Troilus because she wanted to believe it and because the code declared jealousy indicative of true love. Her delicacy, yet fervor, in answering the charge against her endears her to the reader and also shows her greatest weakness, her fatally yielding nature under stress of pity. In this very weakness lay her greatest claim to womanliness, for her surrender was due to tenderness and her anxiety to prove to her lover the very thing about which he had expressed doubt.[15]

And when she ultimately yielded to Troilus's pressures, she is automatically bound by the rules of courtly love. Since marriage does not come into consideration in courtly love, they must keep their love secret, and be deadly loyal to each other whatever may hap. But Criseyde proved to be more of a woman than a courtly lady love by yielding to necessity and Diomede, once she lost all hopes of going back to Troilus's arms in doomed Ilium. Love to her consists not so much in fulfilling the requirements of the code as in the warm embrace of a strong young man who can give her physical and emotional security in that war-ridden world. Her love for Troilus does not continue to hold water in their separation, and she is so much in need of someone to protect her, seeing that of all women she has the most fearful heart. It is a pity that Chaucer has been misunderstood through the ages as being unfair to women, when in fact he shows such understanding of feminine psychology. In making Criseyde look upon love in the carpe diem spirit by which to love to the 'very edge of doom' is sheer imprudence, Chaucer directs his satire on the rules of courtly love which condemn the action of Criseyde. She is the adulterous woman whom the Jews brought to Jesus for condemnation. She thus anticipates the invective of Lear on human justice:

> Thou rascal beadle, hold thy bloody hand.
> Why dost thou lash that whore? Strip thy own back;
> Thou hotly lusts to use her in that kind
> For which thou whip'st her.
>
> (4.6.160-63)

Shakespeare's Hector is a true foil to Chaucer's Criseyde by reason of the contrast between the former's loyalty to the code of chivalry (earning him an undignified death) and the latter's defection from the code of courtly love (earning her a bad name). His ideal of love gone, Troilus has nothing more to live for. But it is not the character of Criseyde that Chaucer blames for the lovers' tragedy. In fact, it is in the Greek camp that Criseyde experiences the bitter battle of loyalty. Her failure to stand the test of love is the Dantesque 'sin of the intellect',[16] an existential duplicity of trying to bridge two opposing worlds. She has 'made a mess of love' by coming short of her ideal of true love. The story of Troilus and Criseyde is the story of passionate and dedicated lovers in a world where love is recognized merely as convention and play—an action subject to time and social convenience.

C.S. Lewis marvels at how "Chaucer can so triumphantly celebrate the flesh without becoming either delirious like Rossetti or pornographic like Ovid".[17] The difference between Lawrence and Chaucer, Lewis seems to point out, is that the former seeks an impossible pure and abstract sexuality whereas the latter seeks to unify the ideal of courtly love and wholesome marital sex. *The Canterbury Tales*, with its panorama of medieval literary forms, becomes at once the vehicle for Chaucer's advocacy of passionate love in marriage. The strongest protest against the failure of medieval code of ethics to integrate love, sex and marriage comes through the complaints of the Wife of Bath, who sees the marriage institution as no place for loving. Hers is a desperate longing for "sexual fulfillment and happiness, something always condemned by authoritative Christian tradition".[18] Just as the economics of marriage separates love and sexuality, "downgrading and dehumanizing sexual relations," even so the Wife "presents her own sexuality in terms of an impersonal force, and a sexual organ quite abstracted from the complete human being, body and soul".[19] This longing for a fuller relationship in marriage constitutes Chaucer's main theme in some of the stories told by the pilgrims.

The Franklin, the Merchant, the Miller, the Reeve, all come out with tales which have significant bearings on the problems of love, loyalty and marriage. While most of the tales draw laughter at the expense of the marriage institution, courtly love is laughed to ridiculousness in the Nun's Priest's tale of a vain cock and his harem of seven hens "for to doon al his plesaunce." The Wife of Bath has characteristically compromised human frailty with her ideal of easy virtue:

> But of no nombre mencion made he,
> Of bigamye or of octogamye;
> Why shoulde men spake of it vileinye?
>
> (Prologue—*Wife of Bath*, 32-34)

The proud display of Chauntecleer's and Pertelote's virtues, and their mutual admiration show courtly love as silly and ridiculous. Just as the glory of Medieval code of chivalry was being trampled in the dust and sweat of the bitter wars of English succession, so also was the code of courtly love finally desecrated and rendered obsolete. It remains to be answered how far Chaucer succeeds in unifying love and marriage; but his contribution to the process of refining the conception of love is not to be denied.

Chaucer has painted in *The Canterbury Tales* a bright canvas depicting 'the very age and body of the time' which no historical narrative can substitute. But that world and the system which sustained it was irrevocably breaking up. "The leaven of the Renaissance is already at work".[20] Economic prosperity, the rise of the gentry with their monetary power, invention of gunpowder, rising political awareness, weakening of Papal power and a decline in religious convictions, intermittent wars and intrigues, combined to disintegrate the medieval ideals of chivalry and code of honour, leveling the situation of man to that of

> A poor player,
> That struts and frets his hour upon the stage.
>
> (*Macbeth*, 5.5.24)

In contrast to Chaucer's happy pilgrims, Shakespeare's characters, even the happiest of them, are people who have learnt to say either that men

> Are as the time is; to be tender-minded
> Does not become a sword. (*King Lear*, 5.3.32)

or that life's puzzles may best be solved by Time, while man is left to choose either "to be or not to be"—an ambiguous philosophical jargon that may be stretched from the gates of heaven to a dew-drop of non-being.

A new age was being born: an age of change and upheaval in which received ideas were examined, and ideals questioned. Doubts and skepticism, hitherto heretical, went at large in the name of science and progress. Suddenly, Renaissance man found himself free—free to search the universe for fresh values to give legitimacy to his actions. Shakespeare came to London which was bustling with significant political events: troubles at sea, plots and conspiracies in the land. In spite of the picture of 'merry England' Elizabethan life, for many, was "nasty, brutish, and short".[21] The gleam of the axe was a matter-of-fact necessity of social and political welfare. It was said of James I that he "was constantly afraid of assassination and wore quilted clothes to defend himself from a dagger's thrust".[22]

But it was not the dagger only which shortened life in the realm of Albion. Wars and pestilences apart, even peace and prosperity did not conduce to longevity. Ivor Brown tells us:

> The ways of eating and drinking in Tudor England were not conducive to long sustenance of health...the heaviness and monotony of the feeding was a handicap to longevity.[23]

It is very likely that Shakespeare viewed "too festive occasions" and debauchery with distaste, since we seldom find him treating them generously in his plays. Except Falstaff, few other characters are given to drunken revelry. Sir Toby Belch might leave drinking if Maria kept her wits; and Cassio is conscience-stricken, though being put on by Iago,

> O, I have lost my reputation! I have lost the immortal part of myself, and what remains is bestial...O thou invisible spirit of wine, if thou hast no name to be known by, let us call thee devil!...O God, that men should put an enemy in their mouths to steal away their brains! That we should with joy, pleasance, revel and applause, transform ourselves into beasts!
>
> (*Othello*, 2.3.255ff.)

Drinking and revelry in Shakespeare's plays are invariably the pastime of Fools and supplementary characters as an additive to their comic function. This life of debauchery and unrestrained animal impulse had other consequences which Shakespeare held as the direst enemy, namely the abuse of sex leading to destruction of the body and spiritual hell, as in *Sonnet 129*. Moral and physical diseases worked like teammate to cast a gloomy shadow over the Tudor landscape wherein the more sensitive souls perceived the skeleton beneath the external gloss and polish of a new national enthusiasm. The personal grief of Keats's *Ode to a Nightingale*—

> Here, where men sit and hear each other groan;
> ... ...
> Where Beauty cannot keep her lustrous eyes,

seems to be less universal than such lines written by Thomas Nashe during the plague of 1593:

> Adieu, farewell earth's bliss,
> This world uncertain is:
> Fond are life's lustful joys,
> Death proves them all but toys,
> I am sick, I must die.
> Lord, have mercy on us!
>
> Rich men, trust not in wealth,
> Gold cannot buy you health;
> Physic himself must fade,
> All things to end are made.
> The plague full swift goes by.
> I am sick, I must die.
> Lord, have mercy on us!
>
> Beauty is but a flower
> Which wrinkles will devour;
> Brightness falls from the air,
> Queens have died young and fair,
> Dust hath closed Helen's eye.
> I am sick, I must die.
> Lord, have mercy on us!
>
> (*A Litany in Time of Plague*)

The transience of life and happiness which appear to us as a matter-of-fact truism was felt by Shakespeare and his contemporaries in their bones and nerves; it was a preoccupation of the poets and writers almost amounting to an obsession. The Elizabethan mind bent on taking life at full tilt in all its variety and promises was inimical to such inconsistency apparent before their very eyes. "The Sea of Faith" had given Medieval Christendom an anchor to hold in port the beaten bark of the human soul in the 'sea of life'. To Yeats, speaking for the twentieth-century man—beyond faith,

> Man is in love, and love what vanishes.
> What is there more to say?[24]

It is a question Shakespeare and his contemporaries were compelled to answer whether Renaissance humanism could finally come to terms with human limitations or find a synthesis of the two disparate world views. A man of the old order, a victim of the new, Gloucester puts the blame elsewhere:

> As flies to wanton boys are to th'gods—
> They kill us for their sport. (*King Lear*, 4.1.37-38)

while a younger man, Kent rationalizes:

> It is the stars,
> The stars above us, govern our conditions. (4.2.33)

But when no 'visible spirits' from the heavens come to "tame these vile offences", Gloucester is taught by his be-wised son, Edgar:

> Men must endure
> Their going hence, even as their coming hither.
> (5.3.9)

Whether he chooses 'to be' like Tamburlaine, or refuses 'to be' like Richard II, the forces against him do not seem to care. But there is a third choice, which is to 'let be'—"to take those things for bird-bolts that you deem cannon bullets",—to bear

> Affliction till it do cry out itself
> 'Enough, enough' and die. (4.6.75)

T.S. Eliot thinks that Shakespeare was influenced by Senecan stoicism, pointing out that stoicism afforded the Elizabethans a refuge from the hostility of the time.[25] The stoicism of the philosopher dismisses the old reliance on Providence, and his resistance is unconditional in contrast to the Christian ethics of long-suffering and self-sacrifice in hope of heavenly recompense. But what is the nature of this Shakespearean tensibility? Can we call it a 'life force', an instinctive tenacity of the human will to survive (or a genetic impulse to life), an immortality syndrome? The reverse of Hamlet's aversion to death and uncertainty is love of life and consciousness. For Hamlet, life has no more loveliness, since beauty itself is false. The humanistic apotheosis of man convinces him not. His universe becomes

> a foul and pestilent congregation of vapours.
>
> (2.2.300)

Othello lacks the courage to live in the dark chaos he has unleashed by putting out the 'light' of love. For in Desdemona's death he and we witness the wasting of an "affirmation of our highest values".[26] Desdemona's love takes on the image of untainted humanity because of her innocence (not just in the sense of blamelessness, but a blissful childlike incapacity to think evil). It is this essence in her that Othello loved. It is not so much the loss of conjugal loyalty that so maddened him as it is the loss of his life's vision of spiritual reality. Without this light, having seen it, the world is an empty vale of darkness. We see in Cordelia's death an ideal, tantalizingly real, dissolved by the impersonal exactitude of the 'wheel' come full circle, not only for an Edmund or a Mortimer, but as too fairly for a Mamillius or an Ophelia. Jan Kott twists the knife even more excruciatingly by clearing the stage of everything that man values, leaving a naked, nameless entity, thrown from nowhere, as Beckett's absurd people are.[27] Prof. Sukanta Chaudhuri notices this existential dilemma in Shakespeare too:

> The death of Cordelia gives the final negative answer to the debate on heaven's justice that runs throughout the play. Moral forces seem to have no validity outside mankind...divine mercy has ceased to be an operative force. The moral centre has passed within man.[28]

This shifting of the burden of life from external Providence to man himself has always been the subject of modern philosophy from humanism through nihilism to the modern

Babel, a situation satirically illustrated in the following parody of Creation:

> In the beginning, God created the earth, and he looked upon it in His cosmic loneliness.
>
> And God said, 'Let Us make creatures out of mud, so mud can see what We have done'. And God created every living creature that now moveth, and one was man. Mud as man alone could speak. God leaned close as mud as man sat up, looked around and spoke. Man blinked. 'What is the purpose of all this?' he asked politely.
>
> 'Everything must have a purpose?' asked God.
>
> 'Certainly,' said man.
>
> 'Then I leave it to you to think of one for all this,' said God. And He went away.[29]

That Shakespeare shared with his contemporaries a common literary and philosophical atmosphere, the prevalence of certain themes and conventions has shown clearly, though his treatment of those recurring themes may differ from or even improve upon those of his contemporaries. A writer, such as Shakespeare, working under the strong necessity to accommodate popular taste and his own pockets while keeping low under the searchlight of religious and political sentiments, should have been under no small pressures of conflicting loyalties either to his conscience or to the corporate interest. The choice could be a costly one, as Sir Thomas More proved. That Shakespeare succeeded professionally speaks for his exquisite mastery in manipulating general opinion—apart from the artistic attributes immanent in his works. His plays treat of kings and queens and noblemen, fictitious and historical. But none seems to offend by proximity to living situations. This is because of the impartial magnanimity with which the dramatist has created and handled even the worst of villains. For Shakespeare seems to believe firmly in the innate goodness of man, and in his capacity to develop his highest faculties—love and reason, the attributes of God himself. He was infused, as much as Spenser or Sidney (but not as violently as Marlowe), with the Utopian dreams of Renaissance humanism. But he was also filled with the vision of erring humanity. To 'hold the mirror up to nature' he could not use (as others do) the moral or eschatological scissors to slice humanity with, but he must assume the role of the Creator who left his voluble creation to reason out a purpose in the mystery of existence. Anyone reading Shakespeare has therefore to start from this zero of notional innocence.

The presence or preponderance of the love motif and its potential for counteracting the ravage of time will identify Shakespeare's works with the rest of the literature of sixteenth and seventeenth century England. But there is significant departure from the convention of love poetry in Shakespeare's treatment of love, particularly the absence of such topics as 'carpe diem' and 'carpe florem'—the encouragement to seize present pleasure, and his 'characteristic defiances of Time'.[30] And in his study of Love Shakespeare has broken down the walls of neo-platonic abstraction and the Petrarchan apotheosis of his mistress, approaching rationally the reciprocal love of two individuals in a harmonious blend of conjugal union and social amity. Love in Shakespeare does not elevate the sexual act to the spiritual union: as neither is true by itself alone. The rejection by Shakespeare of the courtly convention of treating love as almost an end in itself could have come naturally from observing the consequence of 'gathering rose-buds' with no better purpose than the satisfaction of doing so. It is the failure of conventional European love poems to achieve the desired union through the flesh which have lent such force to the idea of Plato on Love, an idea which should actually have been developed as an aesthetics and not as a study of human relationship between the sexes. Yet the ideas of Plato concerning Love, by its affinity to the Christian ideals of Love, had a relevance to the post medieval Christian world feeding lustily on the wisdom of pre-Christian civilization. Plato's identification of Love with the desire for the perpetual possession of the good as a means to attain happiness was made subservient to the traditional concept of a well-ordered harmonious universe, as neatly put by Emily Pearson:

> The cohesive element of the Platonic love doctrine as it developed in the Renaissance, consisted of three essentials: the power of love which unites the universe, the passion of human life, which unites man and woman, friends, countrymen, fellowmen; and the divine religion which unites the soul with the deity.[31]

A Florentine teacher of Platonism, Marsilius Ficinus (1433-99), adopting the leading ideas of St. Augustine, syncretized pagan and Christian thoughts in an attempt to win back the minds of those alienated from Christianity presumably by the latter's ascetic demands.[32] But a definite statement of a theory of love was made by Lorenzo de' Medici, the grandson of Ficino's patron, Cosimo de' Medici:

> In the relations of the sexes, love must be limited to one object, and that forever. Few lovers can observe this constancy, and few women can command it; for, in addition to charms of the body, a woman must have a cultivated mind, grace, elegance, suavity of speech, and good sense, and fidelity. Beauty and the eyes gave birth to love; but if beauty fade, other graces remain which are not less dear to the heart. The senses open the door to love, but the soul must cherish a like sacred fire, and become purified by it. Such qualities must be directed by sensibility of heart, and appreciated by elevation and generosity of soul. When two persons meet under such conditions, she becomes more beautiful of soul, more wise, more happy in her affections; and he, to please her, must try to excel in virtue and beautify his soul, that he may emulate her moral and corporeal grace.[33]

It is apparent that the medieval courtly ideal of woman as the personification of love and beauty had found its way into the minds of the neo-platonists, showing that man's finite mind cannot love a mere abstraction of beauty, but needs a concrete, tangible object and feelings to inspire and give birth to his latent power of love. Cardinal Bembo (1470-1547) advanced the idea of love by approximating love of woman to love of God as she is "the nearest approach to divine beauty".[34]

The idea gained momentum and came to a climax in Firenzuola who identified bodily beauty with beauty of soul. It was he who set forth a detailed catalogue of female beauty, just as Castiglione had done for the Courtier—luxurious soft hair, dark full eyes under a serene forehead; a nose slightly impudent yet sensitive; well-shaped lips showing not over six upper teeth in repose, and so on.[35] Significantly enough, the works of Bembo discuss various kinds of love, including vulgar or dishonest love and virtuous or honest love.[36] Celebrations of these two disparate forms of love existed side by side in the little court circles of Renaissance Italy. And it is from thence that Elizabethan poets took the fashion, adapting the lighter vein of Italian thought to suit the more contemplative temperament of their native literature.

Deeply religious and impeccably moral, Sir Philip Sidney (1562-86) created a sensation by his exemplary life, his glorious death, and by his Sonnets published in 1591 as *Astrophel and Stella*, a work which brought the spirit of Petrarch to his countrymen. The epitome of the courtly ideal of an accomplished young man, on whose shoulders "the mantle of Petrarch had fallen," Sidney was "born with a philosophy of love".[37] For Petrarch and Sidney 'true love' was indeed an ideal which remained virtuous and pure in its unattainable, spiritual state. And it was no small attainment for the poet to arrive at this celebration of the universal beauty after the strong desire to possess the particular beauty has been overcome. *Astrophel and Stella* is a record of the poet's struggle inside himself with physical longing—to give way to which is but to forfeit the ideal of beauty immanent in the beloved. For the nature of love is such that the ideal cannot be separated from the practical, which the purely idealist cannot subscribe to.

So while thy beauty draws the heart to love,
As fast thy virtue bends that love to good.
But, ah, Desire still cries, 'Give me some food'.

(LXXI)

Either the flesh or the spirit must win, or go back to the sensual hypocrisy of medieval courtly love. For Sidney the victory of the ideal is celebrated in the following renunciation of temporal Love:

> Leave me O Love, which reachest but to dust,
> And thou my mind! Aspire to higher things:
> Grow rich in that which never taketh rust:
> Whatever fades, but fading pleasure brings.
> ... ...
> And thinke how evil becometh him to slide,
> Who seeketh heav'n, and comes of heav'nly breath.
> Then farewell world, thy uttermost I see,
> Eternall Love, maintaine thy life in me.[38]

This ascetism, this transcendence, this renunciation, this idolatry in love exemplifies the essential weakness of the early Elizabethan Renaissance in its failure to face the realities of life; its neo-platonic ideal being a combination of the classical worship of Beauty as the Love incarnate and the ascetic Christian virtues. Such romantic idealism can never relate itself to the mundane facts of visible existence, but must avoid at all cost whatever may prevent the attainment of this philosophical heaven: earthly career and advancement as well as the enjoyment of love in the body. Herein is Shakespeare's great contribution to the Renaissance that he was able to harmonize the ideal and the hard realities of life—a feat no ordinary imagination can perform.

But whereas Shakespeare examines Love in the social and political framework in which morality is measured on the scale of its applicability to universal good, Edmund Spenser (1552-99), like Sidney, insists on the necessity of making morality the end of Love by dignifying his conception of love. He, however, does not contemn love of body as antithetical to love of soul as Sidney does, but reconciles the two in a happy fusion of Platonism and Christianity whereby the true end of Love may be served in begetting beautiful inheritors. This is the original tenet of Plato's dialogue on Love, namely that

> the object of love...is to procreate and bring forth in beauty... because procreation is the nearest thing to perpetuity and immortality that a mortal being can attain.[39]

We may thus see in Spenser a possible mine of ideas from which Shakespeare might draw the matter of his Sonnets. In a beautiful synthesis of Plato's ideas of Beauty and the creation of man after the likeness of God recorded in the book of Genesis, he describes the generation of beauty (in this case man or woman as the subjects of love) as soul emanating from the Godhead, forming the body.

> What time this worlds great workmaister did cast
> To make al things, such as we now behold,
> It seems that he before his eyes had plast
> A goodly Paterne, to whose perfect mould
> He fashioned them as comely as they could;
> That now so faire and seemely they appeare,
> As nought may be amended any wheare.
> That wondrous Paterne wheresoere it be,
> Whether in earth layd vp in secret store,
> Or else in heauen, that no man may it see
> With sinfull eyes, for feare it to deflore,
> Is perfect Beautie which all men adore,
> Whose face and feature doth so much excel
> All mortal sence, that none the same may tell.[40]

The beauty of the soul which flowers in the bodily form as its very image, therefore, should not be taken at face value, as that visible part is subject to decay, and abuse. But the soul does not take blame for the sin and corruption of the body:

> Nathelesse the soule is faire and beauteous still,
> How ever fleshes fault it filthy make:
> For things immortall no corruption take.[41]

Women (to use concrete terms) should not, however, allow their beauty to be despised for their immoral conduct in love; but should select deserving partners in match to their beauty for husbands. In fact, heaven had originally ordained who should in love be united so that beauty and harmony may be preserved in the universe:

> For Loue is a celestiall harmonie,
> Of likely harts composed of starres content,
> Which joyne together in sweete sympathie,
> To worke ech others ioy and true content,
> Whish they haue harbourd since their first descent
> Out of their heauenly bowres, where they did see
> And know ech other here belou'd to bee.[42]

It is Spenser's significant contribution to love-poetry hitherto torn between erotic and divine love that he has ennobled physical love as a foretaste of heaven's bliss. For once the humanist in him gets the better of the moralist:

> Hart need not wish none other happinesse,
> But here on earth to haue such heauens bliss.[43]

The momentary (perhaps desperate) admission that the sight of earthly beauty appeals stronger to him than the vision of celestial beauty in this Sonnet, together with Donne's *The Extasie*, may have laughed the sterile idealism of Plato to scorn. There the lovers sat upon a flowery bank, their hands and eyes and souls holding communion. And then,

> But O alas, so long, so farre
> Our bodies why doe wee forbeare?
> They' are ours, though they'are not wee, Wee are
> The intelligences, they the spheare.

'Good love' 'grown all minde' might 'forbeare', but the 'subtile knot' must be tied, and 'pure lovers soules' must descend 'T'affections, and to faculties' so that 'Weake men on love reveal'd may looke' to read 'Loves mysteries' in the book of love which is the body.

But Spenser was a poet first, and the need of poetry must be served before the need of philosophy. This was convincingly stated by Prof. Sukanta Chaudhuri:

> The synthesis of 'earthly' and 'celestial' chivalry, erotic and divine love, strains the potential of the medieval material to the utmost.[44]

In making the medieval landscape the setting of his moral allegory, Spenser could not maintain the innocence of the Garden of Adonis without reminding us of the licence of courtly *amour*, the Castle Joyeous, wherein true love has been imprisoned by Busirane till rescued by Britomart who is married love.[45] *The Faerie Queene* might have begun with high hopes of 'Merry England' becoming a reality, had not experience taught him that the struggle for perfection could not simply be concluded as in a fairy tale. And his Fairy Queen was no fairy but a real fiery queen whose virgin flame had singed those who came too near. And those who went adventuring against the forces of invisible enemies were not always rewarded in her court. Life taught the poet the emptiness of an ideal, how even the most favoured fall into displeasure for a word misspoken. The 'fissures' or 'dislocations' are noticed by Gary Waller in his illuminating study of the period:

> Spenser's epic is the most important single poem of the century precisely because it brings so compellingly to our attention the conflicting voices by and against which it was written; it allows us more richly than any other poem of the age to construct those voices which spoke so powerfully to create the hegemony of the Elizabethan regime. *The Faerie Queene* emerges in a cultural space radically crossed by impulses and structures which it vainly tries to discipline, and which over and over at key moments in its unfolding, articulate the ideological struggles of late Elizabethan society.[46]

The logical sequence and appropriate response was to recoil from reality and look elsewhere to build hopes upon. From *The Rvines of Time* to the last Book of *The Faerie Queene* entitled *Mutabilitie*, there are passages showing disorientation with the ways of the world and nostalgic longings for a reality above the sway of Time and Mutability: the eternal, timeless, unchanging city of God. The need to reject and transcend the imperfections of this world is basically incongruous with the spirit of Renaissance humanism that we find better expressed in Shakespeare.

The death of Sidney occasioned a serious contemplation on the subject of mutability in Spenser, echoing a number of Shakespeare's Sonnets on the destructive aspect of Time. In *The Ruins of Time* he brings up a series of pictures of ancient monuments of greatness obliterated by the passage of time. Like Milton on like occasion contemplating the futility of a noble pursuit, Spenser dwells on the trickiness of 'Fortune's ice':

O trustless state of miserable men,
That builde your blis on hope of earthly thing,
And vainly thinke your selues halfe happie then,
When painted faces with smooth flattering
Doo fawne on you, and your wide praises sing,
And when the courting masker louteth loue,
Him true in heart and trustie to you trow.
All is but fained, and with oaker dide,
That euerie shower will wash and wipe away,
All things doo change that vnder heauen abide
And after death all friendship doth decaie.

It is impossible not to think of Shakespeare's possible indebtedness to Spenser in his Sonnets when we read the eighty-nine Sonnets of *Amoretti*, several of which may have likely been reworked by Shakespeare. The following Sonnet may exemplify Shakespeare's possible use of Spenser by its bearing upon Shakespeare's *Sonnet* 60:

One day I wrote her name upon the strand,
but came the waues and washed it away:
agayne I wrote it with a second hand,
but came the tyde, and made my paynes his pray.
Vayne man, sayd she, that doest in vayne assay
a mortall thing so to immortalize,
for I my selue shall lyke to this decay,
and eek my name bee wiped out lykewize.
Not so, (quod I) let bazer things deuize
to dy in dust, but you shall lieu by fame:
my verse your virtues rare shall eternize,
and in the heauens wryte your glorious name.

> Where whenas death shall all the world subdew,
> our loue shall lieu, and later life renew.
>
> (*Amoretti*, *Sonnet* 75)

The poem is only an example of others in Spenser where the poet discovers his desperate yearning

> for stasis, to project truth as unalterable in the face of unpredictability and, in its manifestation in Elizabeth and her Court, as natural, given and unassailable.[47]

The Machiavellian spirit waxed strong in history, and the virtuous poet was poorly shielded against the subtle inducement to rationalize his ideals or simply to throw it away as an illusion in what Gary Waller calls "loss of epic vision".[48] So far as Spenser is concerned, not just his ideals, but his world and his universe on which those ideals take form—a beautiful Utopian universe constructed after the philosopher's own heart—undergo a process of decay in the continual motion of time. An Italian philosopher who was later burned at Rome in 1600, Giurdano Bruno came to Oxford and stayed for two years (1583-85) giving lectures on his 'heretical' philosophy of Nature, which he

> considered as an organic whole which stands in the centre of the picture, and not terrestrial human beings who are *circonstanzie* or accidents of the one living world-substance.[49]

The relevance of Bruno in the present investigation is his idea of Time and Mutability in relation to Man and his idea of existence, which at his time was novel and extremely dangerous. He taught that change with the passage of time called 'mutability' is the essence of reality and the immutable law of the universe. In his decentralized universe nothing remains static; and the happiness man should seek lies in the ever-changing present which alone is available to him for use. Change or mutation, Bruno is saying in effect, is the sign of a living universe whose soul is

> A motion and a spirit, that impels
> All thinking things, all objects of all thought,
> And rolls through all things.[50]

In his *Mutability* Cantos Spenser insisted finally on the eschatological comfort of God's changeless Eternity "That is contrary to Mutabilitie."

The pantheistic naturalism of Bruno's concept of Time and Mutability did not take into account man's instinctive bid to preserve consciousness and identity, or what Otto Rank calls "the will to immortality".

> This 'will to immortality' is our innate sense of connection with life and all its relationships, whether towards ourselves, others or God. A striving for self-perpetuation is inherent in human nature; it is the urge to maintain our individual identity beyond the limitations of the body. We are in conflict with death, and while we cannot overcome it physically, we can do so ideologically.[51]

That, in brief, may be the psychologist's explanation of the conflict between the temporal and the eternal in relation to man's perception of his being. Time, here, is the agent of death and non-being, while eternity holds hope of preservation of being and identity. Philosophy and religion assert a meaning to life; but life does not offer any convincing proof of survival beyond death. For man is part and parcel of the ever-moving universe in the totality of his being in spite of his 'timeless' consciousness crying, "I am not a part of this system, I am an eternal soul imprisoned in this perishable time-consumed essence of dust". Matter is indestructible. The body continues to exist in space-time continuum. But the individual essence, as a communicable unit, has vanished. It is this thought of total extinction which makes death unbearable. The more in human history life offers promises of happiness and pleasure, the stronger is felt the urge to resist, and assert the will against the forces of time and mutability, or even the consequences of one's actions.

In a little book but one of its kind in the exploration of time in the context of literature, S.H. Vatsyayan relates Time and Eternity to the changing and shifting awareness of man towards his own existence in a way which throw significant light on the treatment of time by Shakespeare and Donne.

> The vast and astonishing patterns of change in human history, the wonderful new dimensions opening up before man in *this* world, obscured the dimensions of eternity and led to its decline and gradual collapse. The horizons of eternal life were lost; man began to live more and more in the dimension of human history in this changing world; time began to be experienced more and more as constant change. Not stability but change became the basic value.
>
> Eternity survived as a concept, but only in the religious outlook which increasingly lost its force, function and significance in the context of social and historical actuality. Eternity had become a 'belief', still held but with little correspondence to reality.
>
> Confined to the dimension of history, human life shrank under the oppressive impact of time. Historic time was the only medium in which human life unfolded and fulfilled itself. It depended on one's predilection and attitude whether that direction led to an open future of limitless possibility and creation, or toward a closed future of oblivion and death. But whichever end one foresaw, time confronted man with nothing but relentless change and transitoriness.[52]

Ralegh's unfinished *History of the World*, published in 1614 while he waited for his execution, reveals what some of his earlier poems evinced: a singular skepticism of all human values, together with a grim fatalistic view of history

> with no final eschatological goal, no ultimate consummation. History consists only of the continual vengeance of an angry God until 'the long day of mankind...and the world's Tragedie and time near at an end.[53]

His cynicism amounts to a rejection of life in his *Answer to Marlowe*:

> Thy belt of straw and ivy buds,
> Thy coral clasps and amber studs,
> All these in me no means can move

To come to thee and be thy love.
But could you last and love still breed,
Had joys no date nor age no need,
Then these delights my mind might move
To live with thee and be thy love.[54] (Stanza 6 & 7)

His own life, so fresh in promise and yet so bitter in its fruit, offered no alternative attitude but to see life in history as inexorably moving in a vicious cycle of relentless historical necessity. His little poem, *On the Life of Man*, a sad companion to Jaques's "Seven ages of Man" in *As You Like It*, could well have come from the mouth of Macbeth:

What is life? A play of passion,
Our mirth the music of division;
Our mothers' wombs the tiring-houses be
Where we are dressed for this short comedy;
Heaven the judicious, sharp spectator is
That sits and marks still who doth act amiss;
Our graves that hide us from the searching sun
Are like drawn curtains when the play is done:
Thus march we, playing, to our latest rest,
Only we die in earnest, that's no jest.[55]

But when the end drew near, he found that he could not meet death without even a semblance of belief in immortality, feeling that he must conclude the poem in a hopeful note:

And from which earth and grave and dust
The Lord shall rayse me up I trust.[56]

What this last minute pietism exemplifies is the inadequacy of human assertion of supremacy which recurs continually in the literature of the sixteenth century England, especially the works of Marlowe, Shakespeare and Donne.

For sheer exuberance and strength of passion Marlowe stands out among his contemporaries. His lines breathe freely, naturally and spontaneously. And his heroes embody the virile lust for life and power, love and wealth of their creator's generation almost to the level of comedy. But the essential Marlowe is clearly revealed by these 'supermen' who truly—

perhaps more than even Shakespeare's characters—incarnate the aspiring spirit of the Renaissance humanists. The fact that Marlowe's dramatic heroes are treated as antagonists indicates the dramatist's mature views of life and his independence of thinking which enables him to examine the tenets of popular humanism. For these heroes are generations of the old classical heroes who attempted the impossible, thereby to stand for all times as monuments of man's illimitable reach for the sky. The failures of Marlowe's heroes, instead of humiliating them, ennoble them all the more for their innate humanity in spite of dramatic hyperboles. They differ, however, from Shakespeare's fallen heroes in the purity and concentration of their hubris; there is little conflict in them. It looked as if Faustus is torn between his religious conscience and his humanistic aspiration to unlimited power; but a closer examination of his motives indubitably reveals an essential absence of the painful spiritual laceration of conscience had he truly cared so much for hell or heaven as much as he does for the supernatural power Mephistophilis can give him. From the very onset of the play, one feels the hubris of pride in his flippant skepticism, which not even the success of his conjuring nor the subsequent testimony of Mephistophilis can intimidate. He is drunk, not with desire for knowledge, but with dreams of unlimited power. He is one who, in Donne's words, would "Be more then man, or thou'rt lesse then an Ant".[57] To the Bad Angel's "Be thou on earth as Jove is in the sky", echoing the first temptation of man, he responds with a thrill:

> How am I glutted with conceit of this!
> Shall I make spirits fetch me what I please,
> Resolve me of all ambiguities,
> Perform what desperate enterprise I will?
>
> (Sc. I. ll. 74, 76-79)

Spirits in Elizabethan English means *devils*. Believing in devils, he dismissed divinity only because the devil serves his lust for power. Scripture is specific:

> But every man is tempted when he is drawn away of his own lust, and enticed.[58]

The sin of Faustus as viewed from the moral standpoint, so Prof. Sukanta Chaudhuri points out, is against his own inflexible moral standard culled from the Bible.[59]

Corollary to this revolt against moral order is his revolt against the order of space-time, whose limitations he must overcome by hook or by crook. By revolting against moral order he incurs spiritual damnation; and by revolting against the space-time order he incurs physical disorder: the mutilation of his body.

In contrast to Faustus, Tamburlaine is blissfully unaware of the moral order he upsets, and therefore, is not punished for his actions, however evil they are to the sensibility of civilized society. He only suffers a check to his aspirations and self-delusion at the hands of Death: a force he has always thought of as mere instrument in his hands till it strikes Zenocrate, whose beauty and love has provided the only relief from the evil and havoc swirling in the wake of his conquering chariot. But Tamburlaine is more than a conqueror. He sees himself as the instrument of Providence, "the Scourge of God", who dispenses life and death at his will, and pursues his mission of conquest as a man possessed. And yet Tamburlaine reveals himself more favourably in his love for Zenocrate. Indeed his love for her redeems his inhumanity for its purity and freedom from the taint of lust that often characterizes Marlowe's lovers elsewhere. And it is through her that Tamburlaine discovers humanity, through her that he comes to realize 'the quality of mercy', the vanity of wealth and power as compared to beauty and love, the power of love over the sword, that Love is the light of life (ll. 2996-2976). And, like Othello, when that light dies, no tempering influence on him is strong enough to stay his revenge on the world whose system has failed him. But when the inevitable end comes, he gracefully accepts it just as he has accepted his destiny as 'the Scourge of God', knowing finally that death alone can reunite him with love and his beloved Zenocrate.

Though the English version of Machiavelli's well known work, *Il Principe*, appeared only in 1640, there are clear indications that the Elizabethans were familiar with the 'infamous' policy of this Italian. Whether for good or bad,

Machiavelli has not always been understood as he deserves. He has been severely subjected to moral and religious judgements which are not within the purview of his subject. His reputation as the Devil's advocate seems to have been well established in England as early as 1592, when Marlowe received an admonitory letter from the dying Greene, warning him against "pestilent Machiavellian policy" the latter had seen in some of his plays.[60] Apart from the turbulent life of Tamburlaine, the appearance of Machiavelli's ghost on the stage to deliver the Prologue to *The Jew of Malta* would have had an electrifying effect on the audience. Riding on the wave of national prejudice against the Jews, Marlowe's audience should have been effectively purged of their xenophobia after seeing this overdrawn Machiavellian essence. Barabas is the type of Iago in his consistent will to evil and resourcefulness in finding means to perpetrate others' destructions. Here again the only relief from the stench of evil comes from the loving nature of Abigail.

But when we come to *Edward II*, the word 'love' assumes a different colour. Love between man and man finds healthy treatment in Shakespeare, almost always surpassing love between man and woman. Here, where words like 'amorous', 'bosom', 'lips', 'arms', illustrate the friendship of two men, where two men love each other's company better than their wives' and where kingdom is as dear to a king as a place to 'frolicke' with another man, the word 'love' is no benevolent charm bringing peace and harmony, but is more like a curse which bring enmity and disintegration. But coldness in love is no justification for adultery. Isabella's courtly epithets like 'gentle' and 'sweet' are as prurient. And the Mortimer "Who now make Fortune's wheele turne as he please" may elicit more tragic sympathy without the 'despised' Isabell by his side. Yet his words,

> Base fortune, now I see, that in thy wheele
> There is a point, to which when men aspire,
> They tumble hedlong downe: that point I touchte,
> And seeing there was no place to mount vp higher,
> Why should I greeue at my declining fall?

(Edward II, 2628-2631)

reverberate through the tragic world of Shakespeare like a clarion call of Renaissance humanity to arm itself against the powers of Time and Mutability.

C.S. Lewis has called Marlowe's part of *Hero and Leander* "the most shameless celebration of sensuality which we can find in English Literature".[61] That Shakespeare has failed where Marlowe succeeds—that is, in portraying sensual love—is attributed by Lewis to the latter's relative shallowness which "does not see beyond the erotic frenzy".[62] This eroticism in Marlowe, the fruit of his translation of Ovid's Elegies, consistently reveals the essential Marlowe as much as the unmitigated passions of his monomaniacs seem to project his Renaissance libido for the elusive Eldorado of human aspirations. The dream of Hero to enjoy nuptial love, the unnatural love of Edward II for his minion, the foiling of Abigail's love, the unholy desire of Faustus to be made immortal by a kiss from 'the spirit of Helen', the possessive love of Dido for Aeneas contrary to the will of Jove that he should not stay in Carthage, and the thwarted love of Iarbus for Dido, the mutual attraction between Isabell and the younger Mortimer (which is really a mask for the love of power), and the perfect love between Tamburlaine and Zenocrate make up the canvas of Marlowe's vision of Love. And it is not such an inspiring picture as some of the languages which convey the pictures are, some of which could well have issued from the pen of his illustrious successor:[63]

> Who euer lov'd, that lov'd not at first sight?
>
> Beautie alone is lost, too warily kept.
>
> Maids are not woon by brutish force and might,
> But speeches full of pleasure and delight.
>
> Loue is too full of faith, too credulous,
> With follie and false hope deluding vs.
>
> In such warres women vse but halfe their strength.

And the immortal poem, *The Passionate Sheepheard to his Loue*, with its irresistible call—

> Come liue with mee, and be my loue

has, together with Shakespeare's *Under the Greenwood Tree*, occupied the foremost place in the expression of pastoral happiness. Incidentally, perhaps, the highest compliment to Love may have been paid by Marlowe when he makes the old Nurse in *The Tragedie of Dido*, as she leads away Cupid as young Ascanus, cogitate upon Love:

> *Nurse*: That I might live to see this boy a man!
> How pretilie he laughs, goe ye wagge,
> Youle be a twigger when you come to age.
> Say Dido what she will I am not old,
> Ile be no more a widow, I am young.
> Ile haue a husband, or els a louer.
>
> *Cupid*: A husband and no teeth!

An old song may make us sympathize with the good Nurse:

> *Love knows no season, love knows no clime;*
> *Romance can blossom any old time.*

Marlowe's place in the history of English Drama and the contribution he makes to the development of the nascent study of human personality is not to be subordinated to those of others whose works draw their fame from the rich well of his masterpieces. Perhaps, more than in the works of his successors do we find in his works the raging tempests of conflicting ideals between the old moral and Theo-centric dispensation and the new rational and homo-centric dispensation. His works are landmarks of the new freedom of will that has come to be man's inheritance from the Renaissance in the context of English Literature.

NOTES

1. Neville Coghill, "The Basis of Shakespearean Comedy", in *Shakespeare Criticism 1935-60*, ed. Anne Ridler, Oxford, 1970, p. 14.
2. C.S. Lewis, *Allegory of Love*, OUP, 1975, p. 4.
3. J.T. Noonan, "Contraception: A History of its Treatment by the Catholic Theologians and Canonists", in David Aers, *Chaucer*,

Langland and the Creative Imagination, Routledge & Kegan Paul, 1980, p. 145.

4. David Aers, *op. cit.*, p. 143.
5. *Ibid.*, p. 13.
6. Lu Emily Pearson, *Elizabethan Love Conventions*, London, George Allen & Unwin, 1966, pp. 6-9.
7. David Daiches, *A Critical History of English Literature*, Allied Publishers, (India), 1984, Vol. I, p. 57.
8. *Ibid.*, p. 68.
9. *Ibid.*
10. *Ibid.*, p. 69.
11. *Ibid.*, p. 81.
12. *Ibid.*, p. 82.
13. *Ibid.*, p. 83.
14. Cf. Pearson, *op. cit.*, pp. 14-30; and Emile Legouis, *A Short History of English Literature*, tr. V.F. Boyson & J. Coulson, Oxford, 1968, p. 42.
15. Pearson, *op. cit.*, p. 22.
16. *Ibid.*, p. 25.
17. *Allegory of Love*, *op. cit.*, p. 196.
18. David Aers, *op. cit.*, p. 149.
19. *Ibid.*
20. Arthur Compton-Rickett, *A History of English Literature*, IBH, New Delhi, 1980, p. 66.
21. Thomas Hobbes, *Leviathan.*
22. Ivor Brown, *Shakespeare in His Time*, Thomas Nelson & Sons, 1960, p. 187.
23. *Ibid.*, p. 75.
24. Quoted in Graham Hough, *The Romantic Poets*, B.I. Pub., 1983, p. 172.
25. "Shakespeare and the Stoicism of Seneca", *Selected Essays*, 1927.
26. M. Alexander, *Introduction to Shakespeare and His Contemporaries*, Pan Literature Guides, London, 1979, p. 203.
27. *Shakespeare Our Contemporary*, Methuen, 1981, Chapter on 'King Lear, or Endgame'.
28. *Infirm Glory*, p. 172.
29. Kurt Vonnegut, Jr., *Cat's Cradle*, New York, Dell, 1970, p. 177.
30. J.B. Leishman, *op. cit.*, pp. 23, 99, 100.
31. Pearson, *op. cit.*, p. 42.
32. S.J. Frederick Copleston, *A History of Philosophy*, Image Books, NY, 1963, Vol. III, Pt. 2, pp. 16-17.
33. Pearson, *op. cit.*, p. 44.
34. *Ibid.*

35. *Ibid.*, p. 49 and Appendix Note 20, p. 325.
36. *Ibid.*, pp. 49-50.
37. *Ibid.*, p. 84.
38. *Certaine Sonets*, in 'Works' ed. A. Feuillerat, Cambridge, 1962.
39. *Symposium*, p. 87.
40. *An Hymne in Honovr of Beavtie*, Poetical Works, ed. J.C. Smith and E de Selincourt, Oxford, 1975, pp. 29-42.
41. *Ibid.*, pp. 159-61.
42. *Ibid.*, pp. 197-203.
43. *Amoretti LXXII*, Poetical Works.
44. *Infirm Glory*, p. 92.
45. *Allegory of Love*, p. 341.
46. *English Poetry of the Sixteenth Century*, Longman, 1968, p. 179.
47. *Ibid.*, p. 206.
48. *Ibid.*, p. 209.
49. Coppleston, *op. cit.*, p. 70.
50. William Wordsworth, *Tintern Abbey*, OAEL, Vol. II, p. 149.
51. Harold W. Darling, *Man in His Right Mind*, Paternoster Press, London, 1977, p. 106.
52. *A Sense of Time—An Exploration of Time in Theory, Experience and Art*, OUP, Delhi, 1981, pp. 11-12.
53. Waller, *op. cit.*, p. 126.
54. OAEL, Vol. I, p. 838.
55. *Ibid.*, p. 839.
56. Waller, *op. cit.*, p. 127.
57. *The First Anniversary*, H.J.C.G.
58. *The Holy Bible* (King James Version), James 1:14.
59. *Infirm Glory*, p. 126.
60. Frederick S. Boas, "Is it pestilent Machiavellian policy that thou hast studied?" *Shakespeare and His Predecessors*, Rupa & Co., India, 1963, p. 30 (Footnote).
61. Essay, *Hero and Leander*, included in 'Elizabethan Poetry: Modern Essays in Criticism', ed. Paul J. Alpers, Oxford, NY, 1967, p. 236.
62. *Ibid.*, p. 237.
63. *Hero and Leander*, ed. Tucker Brooke, ll. 176, 328, 419-20, 221-22, 296.

3

Shakespeare's Treatment of Love, Time and Mutability in his Works

And, beyond our eyes,
The human love lies
Which makes all it gazes on Paradise.

P.B. Shelley—"Prometheus Unbound"

The greatness Shakespeare achieved as a poet and dramatist has often been attributed to his universal sensibility which shows itself through his treatment of human nature. It is impossible not to see the genial humour of Shakespeare in treating human frailties as a sharp contrast to Chaucer or Jonson, whose sense of humour may seem to have finer edge. Chaucer's Canterbury pilgrims may have represented the medieval social strata outwardly: each imperfect individual perfectly filling his niche.[1] When Shakespeare wrote his plays he had a much more difficult task in moulding his characters, not only because the feudal social framework had already dissipated. The cosmopolitan nature of Elizabethan England with its rich intellectual and philosophical background should have made his work of "holding the mirror up to nature" as boundless and limitless as nature has in store. It is, therefore, a matter of great credit to Shakespeare that his works have universal and timeless appeal among people of all class and clime.

This poses a persistent question—what makes Shakespeare's men and women so real and authentic? Dryden's introspective Shakespeare and Mrs. Lang's Arcadian boy-Shakespeare[2] need not have been examples of singular temperaments in Elizabethan England. For the 'current of ideas' was flowing fairly in society, needing only nature to select her medium. Keats may have given the nearest approximation of the key to Shakespeare's genius in his psycho-analysis of the poetical character, that

> It has no character—it enjoys light and shade; it lives in gusto, be it foul or fair, high or low, rich or poor, mean or elevated—it has much delight in conceiving an Iago as an Imogen. What shocks the virtuous philosop(h)er, delights the chameleon poet.[3]

S. Homchaudhuri points out the existential affinity of Shakespeare and Keats with the ancient Greeks in their involuntary awareness of "the twin strains of ecstasy and agony."[4] And indeed it cannot be anything short of such magnanimity of self-annihilating awareness of humanity which informs the genius of Shakespeare to create his immortal characters.

Though it is customary to put Shakespeare after Spenser and Marlowe in literary history, the fact must not be forgotten that they were historically contemporaneous, living and writing within the same political, cultural and literary milieu. Not only they, but Donne and Jonson, besides a host of less prominent writers, produced their significant works which mark the period (roughly from Spenser's *Shepheardes Calender*, 1579, to Ralegh's *History of the World*, (1614) as the Elizabethan Literary Renaissance. The literary career of Shakespeare spanning roughly twenty-five years witnessed the making of perhaps the richest literary epoch in the history of a nation; the more significant for it being a period of political and religious turmoil. The varied nature of literary products this age produced is itself convincing indication of hectic changes of ideas and ways of life. To read such works as *The Faerie Queene* (1590-96), *The Spanish Tragedy* (1594), and *Richard III* (1592), and to see them as the products of the same decade must tax the imagination of a twentieth century reader not well informed about the socio-political character of the age. In a certain way, Spenser's *The Faerie Queene* may be seen as the epic of English humanism in its earthly ideal, if we understand Humanism as part of a general movement of secularization "which sought to turn religious ideals and energies towards the amelioration of life in this world and to achieve an order in this life corresponding to the religious vision of man's worth."[5] Yet, sad to say, as already pointed out earlier, the 'strong necessity of time' cannot accommodate the negation of grosser individual needs for such disinterested ideal. Hence, the general tone of popular Elizabethan literature is that of conflict between the concept of universal organic unity and rising individualism.[6]

Shakespeare is the most powerful exponent of this crisis in humanism. Indeed, we may even think of him as sounding the depth of humanism to see whether it can really provide a solution to life's problems in a way satisfying to man. The crises and conflicts Shakespeare dramatized did not, however, take occasions from just the contemporary break-up of moral order and the increasing emphasis on wealth as instrument of power. He had a rich source of the story of human depravity and lust for power, and also of human dignity and capacity for good in the history of his own country and in the writings of other nations. But if there is any single point on which the works of Shakespeare and those of his contemporaries concur, it is in their attitude to Time as the enemy, and celebration of Love as the highest values man can oppose against the bitterness of ill fortune and death.

There ends the similarity. At the same time, when conventional treatment of Love has rejected the excesses of Petrarch and Ovid in favour of the neo-platonic ideal seasoned with Christian humanistic demand for chastity, Shakespeare brought his intensely searching mind to examine the mysteries of Love at grass-root level dispelling myths and taboos from the temple of Love. So zealous is Shakespeare indeed in his dissection of human nature, which Sir Edmund Chambers has called "remorseless analysis" probing "the inmost being of man, and strip him naked", the "temper of the inquisitor" one should shudder at,[7] that there hangs a certain serious sense of gloom over his dramatic world which not even the most jovial clownage can relieve. In fact, whatever happiness and joy that exist in his works appear but as a little evanescent private world inside a hostile universe which is to annihilate it eventually as if it has never been. Such moments—parenthesis in time—are extremely vulnerable and delicately and precariously balanced on the wheel of fortune. The world of lovers or the world where love operates is antithetical to the law that rules the external world, for they are mutually opposed so that the existence of the one precludes the existence of the other. Shakespeare's picture of the external world is one that has gone 'awry' wherein 'the time is out of joint' and 'there is nothing good or bad, but thinking made it so',[8] a savage world of 'strange mutations' in which

> Humanity must perforce prey on itself,
> Like monsters of the deep. (*King Lear*, 4.2.48)

unless there is supernatural intervention. Shakespeare's vision of history, which the present study is anxious to defend from being called pessimistic, is the vision of every sensitive soul in every age and clime. This is the same vision of anarchy as heralded by the Fool in *King Lear*:

> When priests are more in word than matter;
> When brewers mar their malt with water;
> When nobles are their tailors' tutors;
> No heretics burn'd, but wenches' suitors;
> When every case in law is right;
> No squire in debt, nor no poor knight;
> When slanders do not live in tongues;
> Nor cutpurses come not to throngs;
> When usurers tell their gold i'th'field;
> And bawds and whores do churches build—
> Then shall the realm of Albion
> Come to great confusion. (3.2.81-92)

In a world turned upside down, not accidentally, but as the natural order of disorder, the vision of Yeats in his *The Second Coming*,

> Things fall apart; the centre cannot hold;
> Mere anarchy is loosed upon the world,
> The blood-dimmed tide is loosed, and everywhere
> The Ceremony of innocence is drowned;
> The best lack all conviction, while the worst
> Are full of passionate intensity.

has been the watch-word of poets who look for something better in man. In a very typical humanist moment quite out of his nature, Hamlet feels that it is his duty to set the disjointed world aright:

> The time is out of joint, O cursed spite,
> That ever I was born to set it right! (I.5.190)

His parallel view of man—the humanist ideal and what he finds around him—cannot meet in him, until he realizes, not without a bit of sarcasm, that

> Rightly to be great
> Is not to stir without great argument,
> But greatly to find quarrel in a straw,
> When honour's at the stake. (IV.4.53-56)

Is Hamlet's ideal of man vindicated by his subsequent 'bloody' action, or has he merely compromised it by justifying his cause against Fortinbra's (more sensible) campaign? The words 'ideal' and 'honour' too are subjected to severe examination. In *Troilus and Cressida* the ideal is presented as corrupt and false, and honour in the face of war turns to dust. An ideal must have a living purpose, and honour too is empty vaunt without the seal of victory which the villain's poison can steal away. *Troilus and Cressida* ultimately strips humanity bare of the values and hopes that sustain the will to life, and further "denies the presence of virtuous power in man".[9]

By creating a human situation in which man finds himself alone in an indifferent universe ignorant of his presence, whatever meaning or purpose in life that he cherishes crumbling in his grasp, Shakespeare has skillfully cornered his client into admission of his impotence to rise above the tempestuous sea of his fitful existence. It takes the murder of his father and the dishonour of his mother to make Hamlet see through the thin veneer of the beauty of man the "quintessence of dust". Lear has first to be stripped of his royal power before he learnt the nature of true love. The virtue of this stripping is that, after all, man, instead of looking towards the vast empty space whence no help is coming in his direst need, when faith, hope and ideals are only painful reminders of his suffering, has only to realize that he has but only himself and humanity to turn to, which constitutes for him the only reality that he knows within his grasp. Call it *Existentialism* or the like, Shakespeare is vindicating life in this mundane universe, in a manner that man is truly certain of.

But mankind cannot stand too much reality.[10] His pride and his fear would not let him see that he is subject to his own imperfect nature and the external law of mutability. Leontes in *The Winter's Tale*, by a jealousy born of the lack of trust, one of the attributes of true love, lets loose a bitter winter for his love. But *Othello* is the cruelest love story: with none to benefit from the needless suffering. But that insistence too is unjustified against Shakespeare's 'purpose of playing, whose end' is

> to hold, as 't were, the mirror up to nature; to show virtue her own feature, scorn her own image, and the very age and body of the time his form and pressure.
>
> (*Hamlet*, III.2.20-22)

We may shudder at the thought of Desdemona, whose innocence embodies our image of ideal love, sacrificed by a witless glob of a jealous husband. Yet in the light of Helen Gardner's able defence of the heroic Moor we cannot but empathize with him, as much as we do with Gloucester, Richard II, or Henry VI, as a victim of an alien adversary whose motive and stratagem it is beyond his nature to anticipate, or even when it is all over, understand.

It has become a critical commonplace to take *Romeo and Juliet* as showing the vulnerability of love in a world where love is reduced to mere appetite and social convenience. More has to be said of the sacrifice of innocent children for a belated "glooming peace" and statues in gold which are indeed "poor sacrifices"! But there is no "concessions to sentimentality" in

Shakespeare,[11] for that, as much as a strong faith, robs tragedy of its sting.[12] A man of faith not only endures, but 'bears it' beyond 'the edge of doom' with a cry of victory over that ultimate foe, Death. The essence of tragedy is what a man finds to be truth but cannot accept—truth in the unphilosophic term referring to the experience of mortal flesh and blood.

Johnson's criticism of Shakespeare, in view of the innumerable responses it receives, remains a good starting point for the sensitive question it poses. When he says that Shakespeare often "sacrifices virtue to convenience, and is so much more careful to please than to instruct, that he seems to write without any moral purpose", he not merely "betrays some of the prejudices of his age,[13] but does not take into account the fact that Shakespeare was as much an aspiring professional player-dramatist as an artist whose sole need was that people should like his plays. Another failure of Johnson is his insensitivity to the deep moral questions that pervade most of Shakespeare's works. In view of the cynical Italian proverb that 'poets and pigs are not appreciated until they are dead,' Shakespeare enjoyed popularity in life and death is the most authoritative judgement on the value and relevance of his works. He has vindicated his claim in the *Sonnets* to transfix the beauty of his Friend in his "eternal lines".

It is Shakespeare's consistent response to the human predicament revealed in extreme situations: that Love and Beauty—almost always synonymous in Shakespeare—are the only values that can give man happiness. Men tortured by evil they have not anticipated, nor think is the consequences of their own actions, cry to superior powers for revelation of meaning. Job in the Bible was rewarded for his faith in his God. The gods of Shakespeare's characters do not reveal themselves; and to all palpability do not even exist at all. The silence of the gods affects man in two significant ways. To one who has burned his boats, for whom life would never be welcome again even if one were to begin life anew, a man like Macbeth, death holds no terror. Eternal extinction, were it possible, is a welcome relief from the painful jabs of conscience and the hatred of other men.. Othello, were he to be forgiven a thousand times by the Venetian state, will never forgive himself. T.S. Eliot is unreserved in his opinion:

> I have never read a more terrible exposure of human weakness—of universal human weakness—than the last great speech of Othello.
>
> What Othello seems to me to be doing in making this speech is cheering himself up. He is endeavouring to escape reality.[14]

Having seen and possessed the very embodiment of beauty and perfection, and then to part with it for ever is a terrible thing for any man, and more so for a tragic hero that Othello is meant to be.

> But I do love thee; and when I love thee not
> Chaos is come again. (III.3.92-3)

Desdemona had meant for Othello a harbour to his ever wandering life, order in his hitherto adventurous life. And now he has deprived himself like a fool burning his own house of his only heaven. When Antony is told that Cleopatra had taken her own life, his immediate response is, not shock, or surprise, or grief, but the close of an Act in a play or the end of one stage in life:

> Unarm, Eros; the long day's task is done,
> And we must sleep. (IV.14.35)

Antony looks forward to another life of love in another life-dimension. Othello has no such expectation because he has just destroyed his heaven here in life. For Antony, life holds nothing but shame unless he can find a corner of earth where he and Cleopatra may live their love in spite of kingdoms and thrones. His only purpose in living or dying is Love. Like the ever-changing shape of the unstable cloud, his fortune suffers ups and downs. But when he saw Cleopatra desert him in the naval battle, that is when he really felt fear. His despairing cry,

> O sun, thy uprise shall I see no more! (IV.12.17)

also knells the setting of the sun of love. It is love, and not dreams of empire any more, which gives him the strength for battle. When Cleopatra deserts him, when she reportedly has taken her own life, when she sends him word that she lives, Antony's life ebbs and flows, hanging on the name of Cleopatra. She has become his life, and his life is not complete without her. But there is no more time for their love in Caesar's world. The feeling of futility and insecurity for the lovers seems to overwhelm the poet too. *Sonnet 64* and *66* sweep up a vast canvas of human history marred by perpetual injustice and Time's destructions which robs the viewer of the will to life. In this cosmic rubble only one bright gem shines temptingly—Love. And for this gem only, which is not found in Beckett's bare platform, life is asserted and given a meaning and a purpose. It is not for some unattainable philosophical ideal that St Paul urges the worldly Corinthian converts:

> Love never fails...And now these three remain: faith, hope and love. But the greatest of these is love.[15]

The other way in which the gods' silence and indifference affects man in Shakespeare is decided not so much by external compulsion as by the inherent quality of an individual's personality which reveals itself in a remarkable adaptability to varying circumstances without compromising any values. Of course, the ambiguity in the word 'adaptability' has to be taken seriously. For there are more ways to adapt oneself to circumstances than one. Shakespeare's characters are rarely 'types', yet they may conveniently be identified in groups by the ways they respond to their circumstances. At the lowest scale are the functional characters who merely owe their presence to the dramatist's need to put on the semblance of life—soldiers, servants, attending lords and ladies. Not incidentally, however, they serve as touchstones for certain insights into the plots and characters, and also as choruses. These are not personally involved in the weaving of the plot. They are more or less bystanders who grieve and rejoice with the main incidents. The Fools who serve the whims of their overlords play more significant roles. They enjoy exceptional immunity against the displeasure of their superiors by virtue of their office. Turning this to advantage, Shakespeare uses these licensed Fools as the voice of reason or as the conscience of the hero or heroine. They are 'Fools' in the sense that they speak and act with no respect to conventions of social decorum, shooting witty disarming remarks full of commonsense at the destructive passions displayed by their superiors. They serve as safety valves in such critical situations in the play which threaten to blow up before the characters are ripe for the catastrophe or are come to self-realization. They are indispensable when the dramatist's work of perfecting his leading roles is done. Feste in *Twelfth Night* overstays his time only because he plays more than the Fool's part. The wisdom latent in Lear's Fool, the down-to-earth unromanticism of Touchstone, the verbal dexterity of Feste, do more than relieve tension, but in their own way suggest a code of simple ethics which have a primeval quality about it.

Then there are the sharks of Machiavellian breed,[16] who prey single-mindedly on unsuspecting victims. It is possible that a bit of Machiavelli actually goes into the making of Edmund and Iago. But the true Machiavellian thoroughbreds appear in Bolingbroke and Octavius Caesar. These worldly-wise men can turn almost any situation to their advantage. The young and but taciturn Octavius is in true colour of the conquering megalomaniac when in the tent of war with Mark Antony:

> Ant. Octavius, lead your battle softly on,
> Upon the left hand of the even field.
> Act. Upon the right hand I: keep thou the left.
> Ant. Why do you cross me in this exigent?
> Oct. I do not cross you; but I will do so.
>
> (V.1.16-20)

Born to rule and dominate, Octavius takes no second place to anyone. He and Bolingbroke are purely children of situations—the 'strong necessity' of political exigency their licence. They are pillars of strength in their mastery of the game. They play to win, not because they are thrown in and willy-nilly have to follow the current like most people. Close-mouthed, they trust no one but themselves. We do not know their thoughts as they never speak in soliloquy. We do not know whether Henry IV's plan to go to a Crusade to the Holy Land stems from true penitence or from his policy of pulling wool over his subjects' eyes. Yet he and Octavius are no villains. In Machiavelli's book, actions are justified by good, strong rule. The difference between Bolingbroke, whose long reign was spent in crushing rebellions, and Octavius, who won the highest title 'Augustus', apart from difference in political and social background, is that the former comes to power with the help of nobles, about which Machiavelli cautions 'the Prince', while the latter enjoys popular public support in the wake of brutal assassination of their hero. Machiavelli has said:

> A man who becomes prince with the help of the nobles finds it more difficult to maintain his position than one who does so with the help of the people.[17]

In the light of this astute realism King John's desperate

> Withhold thy speed, dreadful occasion!
> O, make a league with me, till I have pleas'd
> My discontented peers!
>
> (*King John,* IV.2.125-27)

and Richard II's repentant admission of blame:

> I wasted time, and now doth time waste me;
> For now hath time made me his numb'ring clock:
> My thoughts are minutes; and with sighs they jar.
>
> (V.5.49-51)

fall on the ears like the sound of the Judge's hammer. If one plays a game, one plays to win, or take the loser's pain. In this power game, it is a fight to the bitter end; and no prerogative of blood or right will stand unless backed by sufficient strength and resourcefulness. For all his saintliness, Henry VI could not turn the tide of politics, having developed a snail-like attitude of hiding from the cruelty of his time and his court. What a contrast he is to his father, Henry V, whose devotion in battle shows him an ideal Christian king—this king who turns despair to hope by an act of the will:

> There is some soul of goodness in things evil,
> Would men observingly distils it out.
>
> (*Henry V, IV*.1.4)

Place beside this Helena's

> Our remedies oft in ourselves do lie,
> Which we ascribe to heaven.
>
> (*All's Well*, I.1.202)

and we almost distil out the essence of Renaissance humanism in its assertion of confidence in the power of man to mould his circumstances. But if we go further and take Edmund's self-legitimizing

> ...men
> Are as the time is; to be tender-minded
> Does not become a sword.
>
> (*King Lear*, V.3.32)

we have a totally opposite type of heroism Richard III displays in his last battle:

> Conscience is but a word that cowards use,
> Devis'd at first to keep the strong in awe.
> Our strong arms be our conscience, swords our law.
> March on, join bravely, let us to it pell-mell;
> If not to heaven, then hand in hand in band to hell.
>
> (V.3.309-313)

Or Macbeth's, "tir'd with all these,"

> I gin to be aweary of the sun,
> And wish th'estate o'th'world were now undone.
> Ring the alarum bell. Blow wind, come wrack;
> At least we'll die with harness on our back.
>
> (V.5.49-52)

Macbeth confesses his insensitivity to any horror, having had too much of it; and Edgar admits his ignorance of the limit to endurance when he meets his blinded father. Macbeth, like Claudius, bars himself from repentance with the fruit of his crime. Others like Gloucester, Lear, Leontes and the Capulets and the Montagues, even the duke in *As You Like It*, learn wisdom through suffering the consequences of their old nature. Lear's self-pity ("a man more sinn'd against than sinning") soon gives way to a deeper realization of others' pitiable conditions with a cry:

> O, I have ta'en
> Too little of this! Take physic, pomp;
> Expose thyself to feel what wretches feel,
> That thou mayst shake the superflux to them,
> And show the heavens more just. (III.4.32)

Love in its native hue is discovered to be the centre of the new order. It would be sheer folly to destroy or renounce it for the old destructive order. So the poet in *Sonnet 66* testifies for love:

> Tir'd with all these for restful death I cry,—
> As to behold Desert a beggar born,
> And needy Nothing trimm'd in jollity,
> And purest Faith unhappily forsworn,
> And gilded Honour shamefully misplac'd,
> And maiden Virtue rudely strumpeted,
> And right Perfection wrongfully disgrac'd,
> And strength by limping Sway disabled,
> And Art made tongue-tied by Authority,
> And Folly, Doctor-like, controlling Skill,
> And simple Truth miscall'd Simplicity,
> And captive Good attending captain Ill:
> Tir'd with all these, from these would I be gone
> Save that, to die, I leave my love alone.

What, then, is the nature of Love whose life and essence Shakespeare takes such pains to infuse and distil in his poems and plays? He gives us a vision of the world which is relatively darkened or brightened not so much by an independently motivated external mutability as by the inward possession of illumination by the light of love or by its deprivation or rejection. The storm in *King Lear* assumes cataclysmic proportion in respect to the inner storms raging within the characters exposed to it. 'The poor naked wretches' whom Lear invokes suffer more in Lear's new-gained empathy than they normally do in their perpetual natural state of poverty, having had nothing better to compare their present lot with. Richard III merely contradicts himself when he rationalizes that the sour sky on the morning of his battle with Richmond also lours upon his opponent. He is awakened by his guilt whereas Richmond is strong in his innocence. The world of tragedy and political competition provide little scope for the growth and exercise of the gentler attribute of humanity that Shakespeare exploits masterfully in the Comedies and Poems. When Love is reduced to mere appetite and political advantage, lovers become selfish, cruel, untrustworthy, self-defeating. Egypt and Rome are antithetical and tend to annihilate each other. The meddling Olympian deities are dismissed in Shakespeare's Troy, and human actions are seen and judged in relation to their immediate efficacy to satisfy individual need. The values held dear by Hector is self-destructive; the 'truth' sworn by Troilus and Cressida fail to stand the test of situation.

Measured against such degenerative moral standard, the nature of love asserted by the poet in his Sonnets seem but idealism characteristic of literary conventions. Against such love that demands proof of sincerity—from Cressida by Troilus, from Hermione by Leontes, from his daughters by Lear—*Sonnet* 116 posits an ideal love

> Which alters [not] when it alteration finds,
> [N]or bends with the remover to remove.

This is 'idealistic' from the viewpoint of the world where love depends for its birth and sustenance on the appearance of beauty, and the word is given the quality of a commodity for bargain wherein its value is estimated on a one-way traffic basis. Love and marriage, considered as social institution, usually carry price tags which both sides of the parties continually wave at each other. Such institutionalized love and marriage more often than not fail to elicit adequate response to the spirit of love. Social morality, viewed independently of an external order bearing upon human existence, may also be reduced essentially to an instinctive revolt against man's innate tendency to destructive self-indulgence. Hence the persistent feeling that Shakespeare is highly sceptical of the stability of human virtues when subjected to the contrary demands of existential circumstances. It, therefore, seems no easy task to formulate a clear-cut Shakespearean attitude to love when there is antithesis between the imaginative ideal and what people do. Neither is it simple to ascertain how many of his lines are written as conventional exercise and how many from philosophical convictions. That Shakespeare achieves mastery of his art through constant practice has been argued convincingly by several critics who have made comparative studies of Elizabethan poets and dramatists.[18] In his discussion on *Hero and Leander* by Marlowe, C.S. Lewis makes a telling comparison between it and Shakespeare's *Venus and Adonis*, works which appeared in the same year, i.e. 1593, in which Shakespeare emerges poorer in portraiture of sensual love for the commendable reason that Shakespeare is out of his element when describing erotic situations.[19] In the same context, Shakespeare's imaginative bias seems better expressed by Cressida, when she, "A woman of quick sense", finds herself so adaptive to fortune:

> Troilus, farewell! One eye yet looks on thee;
> But with my heart the other eye doth see.
> Ah, poor our sex! this fault in us I find,
> The error of our eye directs our mind.
> What error leads must err; O, then conclude,
> Minds sway'd by eyes are full of turpitude.
>
> (V.2.105-10)

which Thersites paraphrases as "mind...turn'd whore."

Shakespeare's observation of life is too well informed to treat love in his works in an Ovidian abandon to the *carpe diem* and *carpe florem* attitude of obsession with the pleasures of love. When Shakespeare comes to grips with the passions of love inspired by sexual attraction his reaction is downright rebellion against his grosser senses. The Sonnets dealing with the *Dark Lady* mirror a more than conventional revulsion from what is to be understood in the poems as the abuse of love, "The expense of spirit in a waste of shame', a mere "uncertain sickly appetite". As Cressida has done, the poet now imputes the sin to the eyes that "see not what they see" "by over-partial looks". *Sonnet 137* is a fitting commentary on the love that thrives on looks such as Cressida's, a connection also made by Kenneth Muir[20] as well as with Doll Tearsheet:

> Thou blind fool, Love, what dost thou to mine eyes,
> That they behold, and see not what they see?
> They know what beauty is, see where it lies,
> Yet what the best is take the worst to be.

This rebellion of the flesh against the will or reason, not unlike what Wordsworth feels in a different context,

> The eye—it cannot choose but see;
> We cannot bid the ear be still;
> Our bodies feel, where'er they be,
> Against or with our will.[21]

naturally leads judgement to error, and

> We are led to Believe a Lie
> When we see not Thro the Eye.[22]

Scriptures says as much—

> For where your treasure is, there will your heart be also.[23]

The poet's treasure, his 'better angel' is now become, like Antony, "the bellows and the fan/To cool" a woman's fiery love, and the poet appears to be drawn moth-wise towards the singeing flame.

> So, now I have confess'd that he is thine,
> And I myself am mortgag'd to thy will,
> My self I'll forfeit, so that other mine
> Thou wilt restore to be my comfort still. *(Sonnet 134)*

A rather far-fetched implication is that the poet offers himself at this sensual altar in the hope of saving his Friend from suffering the infamy of a harlot's curse.

> To win me soon to hell, my female evil
> Tempteth my better angel from my side,
> And would corrupt my saint to be a devil,
> Wooing his purity with her foul pride.

And whether that my angel be turn'd fiend
Suspect I may, yet not directly tell;
But being both from me, both to each friend,
I guess one angel in another's hell:
Yet this shall I ne'er know, but live in doubt
Till my bad angel fire my good one out.

(Sonnet 144)

Yet it seems more than a voluntary surrender when we read *Sonnet 141*:

In faith, I do not love thee with mine eyes,
For they in thee a thousand errors note;
But 'tis my heart that loves what they despise,
Who in despite of view is pleas'd to dote.
Nor are mine ears with thy tongue's tune delighted;
Nor tender feeling to base touches prone,
Nor taste nor smell desire to be invited
To any sensual feast with thee alone;
But my five wits nor my five senses can
Dissuade one foolish heart from serving thee,
Who leaves unsway'd the likeness of a man,
Thy proud heart's slave and vassal wretch to be.
Only my plague thus far I count my gain,
That she that makes me sin awards me pain.

Cressida's heart went with her other eyes to Diomed, and "All's done" for Troilus. When the mind plays pander to the eye—the eye which feeds on external beauty, that beauty becomes prey to desire. Thus in *Sonnet 147*:

My love is as a fever, longing still
For that which longer nurseth the disease;
Feeding on that which doth preserve the ill,
Th'uncertain sickly appetite to please.

Such seems to be the love of Gertrude for the elder Hamlet, the love inspired by Cleopatra. The sum of Shakespeare's attitude to love between man and woman in which sex is understood to be the 'prize' or the natural consummation of love becomes unmistakably clear. And it is here that we find Shakespeare treating love in the Ovidian tradition of portraying love as a cruel god. But Shakespeare never seems to take his eyes off the stark reality of the feeling of guilt and emptiness that follows the pleasure of love, unless when love is enshrined in the sanctity of the marriage vow. But marital love, apart from "the marriage of true minds", is not the subject of poetry.

We have seen the nature of love as practised in the medieval tradition of courtly love. The Elizabethan court crowded with handsome lords and ladies would have presented the watchful eyes of the poet innumerable examples of interesting affairs with dire results. One such affair leading to the murder of one Sir Thomas Overbury is recounted by Ivor Brown.[24] Another interesting anecdote of the irresponsible amour of Sir Walter Ralegh is recorded by James Sutherland.[25] Inconsequential incidents as these give flashes of the Elizabethan courtly romances. It therefore is no small hazard that Shakespeare takes in throwing a dismal light on the levity of the courtly romantic affairs. And it is difficult not to regard the licence of courtly romance as the survival of medieval courtly love stripped bare of all its religious camouflage.

It has been shown by some critics that in *Sonnet 144* the poet is talking not about two people of opposite qualities, but of two kinds of love.[26] Kenneth Muir wisely distinguishes the Poet of the Sonnets from Shakespeare the man, presumably with the object of saving the latter from a dubious reputation were he in any way identified with the imaginative self of the former—a distinction so vital to keep himself from involving in popular controversy. And neither is it impossible to distil out the essence of Shakespeare's concern with love without tracing the biographical relationship between the Sonnets and their author.

When Shakespeare begins writing on the conventional theme of love he takes the popular story of the amorous love of the goddess Venus for the uninitiated youth Adonis. The entire 1194 lines of the poem *Venus and Adonis* (first published in 1593) tell the story of a very un-Olympian goddess falling head over heels in love with a fair youth who turns cold at a mere touch. The main arguments of the poem have been given two divergent interpretations. While traditional view regards Venus as sensual love and Adonis as reason in such enthusiastic enunciation as

> "All the pent-up anger of reason in love then burst forth against lust:
>
> Call it not love, for Love to heaven is fled,
> Since sweating Lust on earth usurp'd his name;
> Under whose simple semblance he hath fed
> Upon fresh beauty, blotting it with blame;
>
> And like a cooling shower in the heat of summer, came the following words:
>
> Love comforteth like sunshine after rain,
> But Lust's effect is tempest after sun:
>
> So Venus is shown as the destructive agent of sensual love; Adonis, as reason in love",[27]

a contrary view is expressed by Alur Janaki Ram.[28] Drawing his inference from neo-platonic views of love which is essentially permissive of sex as procreation, he defends the goddess as reasoned love and imputes the coldness of Adonis to "self-negatory Narcissistic love".[29] He says,

> It is in this role as a pacifies of the martial spirit that she tenders her advice to the young Adonis to hunt milder animals like the hare and the deer rather than the dangerous ones like the boar. Moreover, Adonis's absorption in the hunt of the boar to the neglect of the soft hunt (love) only reveals the lack of co-ordination in him between the amatory and martial elements.[30]

In a singular approach to Shakespeare's plays Marilyn French examines with a sharp insight and clarity the nature of sexual relationship in Shakespeare, using what she calls 'the Gender Principles'.[31] She identifies as 'masculine' the human will to positive assertiveness, independence, establishment of law and order, the aspiration for permanence, the ultimate goal to transcend nature and ensure the continuation of the human race and its felicity.[32]

> The masculine principle is thus profoundly threatened by and antagonistic to impulses towards acceptance of simple continuation, of present pleasure, of surrender

> to mortality. These impulses are associated with the feminine principle, which is identified with nature. Defying the power of nature, the masculine principle is the standard of hu(mankind), and identifies the human with the male.[33]

This feminine principle is further split into 'outlaw' and 'inlaw' aspects. The outlaw claims both the masculine and feminine dynamism of killing and of giving birth, and is opposed to the masculine sexuality of possession and rape. It tends to disintegrate and annihilate the masculine structure of order and harmony, and "sees the end of life as pleasure".

> Pleasure of all sorts, but especially sexual pleasure, is a threat to the masculine principle, the energies of which must be directed towards transcendent goals.[34]

It then appears that Shakespeare, in order to give us a wholesome picture of love, must find a synthesis of 'the amatory and martial elements' in love.

The primacy of reason in the inner hierarchy of the soul, which underlines the neo-platonic idea of man as the image of God, has strongly decided Shakespeare's interpretation of love, so much so that passionate love at the expense of reason is seen as evil by Shakespeare.

> My reason, the physician to my love,
> Angry that his prescriptions are not kept,
> Hath left me, and I desperate now approve
> Desire is death, which physic did except.
> Past cure I am now reason is past care. (*Sonnet 147*)

When love has for its object the opposite sex whose beauty and use craves possession as the fulfillment of love, reason is assailed and it becomes

> ....the bawd to lust's abuse!
>
> (*Venus & Adonis*, I. 792)

The feeling is universal. The granting of the body's use is taken for granted as the surrender of love and reason, 'the expense of spirit'. Iago could never have made Othello doubt Desdemona's fidelity except by the sexual innuendos with which he conjures up a mental picture of adultery, and Othello swallowed the bait, hook, line and sinker, as if the sexual act were all that there is in his knowledge of love. Hamlet's world is so infected with this sin that he advises Ophelia not to let her beauty abuse her honesty, and to avoid love altogether,

> for the power of beauty will sooner transform honesty from what it is to a bawd than the forces of honesty can translate beauty into his likeness. This was sometime a paradox, but now the time gives it proof.
>
> (III.1.111-15)

The frustration of the poet of the Dark Lady Sonnets can be understood on the plane of a deceptive ideal in this popular Christian hymn which alludes to the ordeal of Tantalus;

> I tried the broken cisterns, Lord,
> But ah, the waters failed;
> E'en as I stoop'd to drink they fled,
> And mock'd me as I wailed.[35]

Love has opened the poet's eyes to a vision of beauty the possession of which in sensual terms often proves to be illusory, bringing in to the civic personality a kind of civil war in which, to use Brutus's words,

> ....the state of man,
> Like to a little kingdom, suffers then
> The nature of an insurrection.
>
> (*Julius Caesar*, II.1.67)

And since it is in the nature of an insurrection to reject the voice of the other faculties of man's sensual nature, the poet's pilgrim-love thirsting for a spiritual and physical satisfaction finds itself betrayed of its sweet and satisfying prize. One cannot help giving superlative encomium to our poet for his uncanny insight into the mystery of man's unique personality, especially the indivisible nature of physical and spiritual essences which no other writer seems to grasp as honestly as Shakespeare. This difficulty of separating the dual identities of man eventually results with our poet in a decentralization of the self, as observed by Waller:

> ...the 'I' of Shakespeare's sonnets is never stable. It is not the Wordsworthian egotistical sublime or the collective 'I' of medieval hymn or Anglo-Saxon elegy. It is a shattered, decentred voice that searches in vain for stability, as in *Sonnet 75*.... The 'I' is aware only of a lack, which has set desire in motion; it articulates this lack by inserting itself in language, which serves only as a further decentring, as it moves along an endless chain of signification, unable to capture the derived plenitude of significance it attributes to the object of desire.... The Cartesian ego, fifty years later, would try desperately to pin down some unassailable centre to the experience of "I". Shakespeare's sonnets, like Donne's, show the futility of the attempt. The 'I' strives to constitute itself a basis for identity, coherent, and primordial, as a source of order and control, and finds itself always already a function of an endlessly frustrating plethora of differences while producing the illusion of autonomy and control.[36]

The crux of the situation lies in the incompatibility between the two natures of man in whom the harmony of organic unity between the 'various elements' has been jarred out of tune. It is a long and tortuous path full of briars and thorns from the opposite ideals of love and lust to the harmony of all the elements the humble and humbled characters attain in the final plays.

What, then, is the flaw in the love which looks for its consummation in the sensible experience of the sexual act which in itself constitutes the ultimate, the climax, the purest joy that flesh can attain short of spiritual ecstasy transcending consciousness of physical existence? In Shakespeare and Donne the rejection of love on the plane of sanguinary experience come neither from moral considerations of Christian pietism, nor from the neo-platonic refinement of the concept of love as ideal beauty. Theirs is an independent, down-to-earth examination of the intrinsic quality of the love-life of men and women in the natural pattern in terms of its efficacy to give the highest possible happiness to man. And we all know, but know still better with *Sonnet 129* that sexual orgasm as an end of loving is a big lie. Man as male, woman as female, fail utterly to satisfy the longing and desire of the partner. The best of them could only but make hungry

> Where most she satisfies. (*Ant. & Cleo.* II.2.242.)
>
> As if increase of appetite had grown
>
> By what it fed on. (*Hamlet* I.2.144-5)

The question of Shakespeare's assimilation of the ideas of Plato concerning love remains a critical contention. And it would be futile to look for absolute arbitrament in terms of total assimilation or total rejection. The following points from Plato's *Symposium*[37] may be set up by which Shakespeare's indebtedness or otherwise can be measured:

1. It is Love who creates Peace among men, and calm upon the sea, Rest for the winds from strife, and sleep in sorrow. (p. 71)
2. It is Love who empties us of the spirit of estrangement and fills us with the spirit of kinship. (p. 71)
3. Love is in love with what he lacks and does not possess. (p.78)
4. Love is a great spirit whose function, as any spirit's is, is to interpret and convey messages to the gods from men and to men from the gods. (p. 81)
5. Love must be distinguished from the object of love which is beauty, by which is implied that Love needs not be necessarily beautiful externally. (p. 83)
6. Love is a desire for the perpetual possession of the good. (p. 86)
7. The object of love is not beauty, but to bring forth in beauty since procreation is the nearest thing to perpetuity and immortality that mortal being can attain. It is in order to secure immortality that each individual is haunted by this eager desire and love. (pp. 87, 89)
8. Love progresses from the love of physical beauty in the person of a human being and beget noble sentiments.

> But this leads to universalization, and the desire to possess a particular person cannot remain constant, leading to infidelity. But love of a particular person leads to the discovery that beauty of soul is more valuable than beauty of body. When the eye of Love is opened at last to the beauty of inner harmony, the entire world of science becomes a worthy object of love. It is by such steps of examples of beauty that Love finally discovers eternal and absolute beauty which is not beautiful in part, but as a whole. (pp. 92-94)

The will to individual perpetuation through procreation with its propensity for epicurean indulgence often defeats itself and robs itself of the happiness to be derived from the noble act. The urge to possess the beautiful forever may be noble on the philosophical plane, but hardly ever so on the plane of carnal sexuality. That Plato refuses to look on love as sensual and his praise of Socrates' self-control may imply a negative attitude to the epicurean aspect of love. But Plato may be less concerned with the sociological value of love than he is with it as a philosophical concept. Shakespeare's concern with love is nothing if not sociological. Whereas Plato dismisses sensual love as not worth the thought—at most the enemy to philosophical pursuit, Shakespeare takes it seriously, explores it, and suffers traumatically the emotional and intellectual pressures created by conscience and disillusionment of an ideal. The Poet of the *Sonnets* feels like a baited animal trapped by a false fairy, a 'dame sans merci', the *femme fatale*, the female spider and the Platonic antagonist. The poet feels himself compromising his ideals of love because his eyes have been blinded by Love to love what his reason finds unworthy of it. The final numbers of the *Sonnets* are sad records of the poet's admission that philosophical ideals cannot stand the assault of the body's urge to possess and annihilate the passions.

Any attempt to interpret the Sonnets presupposes the original order of their composition, which in the absence of sufficient biographical details inevitably becomes an open critical battleground. Whether Shakespeare 'unlocked his heart' in these Sonnets or he was writing in a highly developed conventional mode on a popular subject is still a matter of subjective enquiry of the internal evidence. The present study does not open itself to either view, but finds it worthwhile to distil out the essence of each Sonnet dealing with the topic under study, and to present as originally as possible the poet's responses to the experience of love in the context of life, time and society.

In *The Symposium* Plato recounts a half ludicrous anecdote concerning Socrates through the mouth of Alcibiades:

> The Socrates whom you see has a tendency to fall in love with good-looking young men, and is always in their society and in an ecstasy about them. (Besides, he is, to all appearances, universally ignorant and knows nothing). But this is exactly the point in which he resembles Silenus; he wears these characteristics superficially, like the carved figure, but once you see beneath the surface you will discover a degree of self-control of which you can hardly form a notion, gentlemen.[38]

Alcibiades goes on to disclose the unsuccessful trial he made on Socrates to break this self-control, proving him a real philosophical lover of beauty. Such love of beauty (if one may side-step the controversial biographical implication of Shakespeare's wooing of patronage on the conventional level) and the desire to have it undiminished by age or by change of affection we find in the Sonnets concerning a Youth whom the poet has befriended in spite of difference in social status. Since Love inspired by woman cannot always maintain its purity and pitch, and is eventually doomed to decline with the waning of philosophical beauty and familiarity, it comes short of the ideal of perfect love which does not alter with age nor

> ...bends with the remover to remove.

Yet this scepticism about heterosexual relationship does not extend to marital relationship and man-woman relationship as prelude to marriage which is the ideal consummation of human love in order to achieve its end. The sanctity of marriage always appears in Shakespeare as security of marriage always appears in Shakespeare as security in love, a symbol of permanence (in the assurance of procreation), the fulfillment of nature's law. Thus, whenever Shakespeare brings lovers together, except for occasional use of bawdy, their relationship never needs to 'go to their bodies' to proof their love: for that is assured by the strength of their love which is strong enough to sustain love

even to the edge of doom.

Throughout his works Shakespeare never elevate the sexual act to the equivalence of love, nor does he make it a necessary complement to 'the marriage of true minds'. Yet to say that Shakespeare is advocating the sterile philosophical 'love' of Plato is to misunderstand Shakespeare's idea of love altogether. The highest blessing that is bestowed on lovers in Shakespeare is the promise of issue. Reference to lovers' desire to be with each other by sexual innuendos usually come from shallower characters like Juliet's Nurse, Iago, Touchstone, and of course the ultimate cynic, Thersites. The nuptial bed is sacred, and is purchased with no less price than the total sacrifice of self in love to the beloved.

Shakespeare comes nearest to Plato's Love in the Beautiful Youth sonnets on the point of the need to propagate beauty. But even here the thought of love's failure to achieve constancy and permanence gets the better of the poet, so that much of the force of the Sonnet is spent on the desperate attempt to arrest the passage of time—the dreaded annihilator of temporal realities. The acuteness of the poet's vision never allows him to lose sight for a moment of the constant passing of time. And when the passage of time is mentioned it is always in relation to its function as the remover and the agent of change and interchange of states of things, and not simply in terms of lost opportunity or the movement of the dial's hands. *Sonnet 15, 30, 60, 64, 65, 73* share with the sceptical utterance of Prospero on the 'insubstantial pageant' of spirits a discomforting vision of a naturalistic universe which does not take man into account. The vision is pervasive, and the poet's felt need to find a centre equally urgent.

When I consider every thing that grows
Holds in perfection but a little moment,

That this huge stage presenteth nought but shows
Whereon the stars in secret influence comment. (15)

And Time that gave doth now his gift confound.
Time doth transfix the flourish set on youth;
... ...
And nothing stands but for his scythe to mow. (60)

Ruin hath taught me thus to ruminate—
That time will come and take my love away.
This thought is as a death, which cannot choose
But weep to have that which it fears to lose. (64)

Only a sensitive soul that looks beyond the glitter of mundane existence such as the poet's can feel the full implications of an amoral existence in an indifferent universe, which Stephen Crane[39] makes to deny any sense of obligation to man. Was Mark Antony, taunted so by Cleopatra to hear the messengers from Rome, sufficiently aware of what he says?

Let Rome in Tiber melt, and the wide arch
Of the rang'd empire fall! Here is my space.
Kingdoms are clay; our dungy earth alike
Feeds beast as man. The nobleness of life
Is to do thus. [embracing] (*Ant. & Cleo.* I.1.33-37)

The situation is not fitting for the metaphysical implications of his words, which may be compared to Prospero's insubstantial pageant speech in the isolation of its inspiration. Yet Antony could not have put their situation in a better light nor could there be a better situation to pit his love-life against the base necessity of temporality. By love, and only by love, man transcends the monotonous necessity of feeding on the decaying rubbish of materialism. King Henry IV has run the gauntlet of this game, and finds the prize not worth the struggle:

The happiest youth, viewing his progress through,
What perils past, what crosses to ensue,
Would shut the book and sit him down and die.
(*Henry IV*, Pt. 2, III.1.54-56)

So bleak and forbidding is this vision without the light of love! The same unrelieved prospect is the landscape of Sonnet 66: a vision of society whose order is turned upside down by corruption. It is a chronicle of ungilded human society envisioned by Lear's Fool already mentioned. Bitterly, the poet utters his premonition of impending danger to his love:

> Against that time (if ever that time come)
> When I shall see thee frown on my defects,
> ... ...
> When love converted from the thing it was
> Shall reasons find of settled gravity:
> ... ...[40]
> To leave poor me thou hast the strength of laws.
>
> (*Sonnet* 49)

In an essay, *Love's Confined Doom*, M.M. Mahood points out the interesting parallel between this Sonnet and the repudiation of Falstaff by Hal in *Henry IV, Pt. 2*. Others[41] think that the Sonnet reveals the failure of love on the level of patronage relationship. In fact, in life the fear is natural, since patrons are not obliged to be true to their admirers as much as the admirer is to the patron. To dismiss the relevance of the poem as a conventional piece is to tear down the very fabric of the essence of literature, as so much of the matter of literature is dependent on conventions.

Again, it is Hamlet's question "to be or not to be" that is expressed in the *Sonnets*. Life does not offer sufficient incentive to the poet for going on towards a "dishonourable graves" except for the thin margin of what little beauty and love there is in the silver lining. When this frail hope vanishes,

> Let me not think on't. (*Hamlet* I.2.146)

Yet Hamlet cannot but "think on't", and it makes him half mad. Man needs a system of values, a philosophy of life, a religion or a religion-surrogate to live by and understand by, in about the same sense that he needs sunlight, calcium or love.

> We need a validated, usable system of human values that we can believe in and devote ourselves to (be willing to die for), because they are true rather than because we are exhorted to 'believe and have faith'.[42]

As much as the poet idealizes on love as in *Sonnet 116*,

> ...it is an ever-fixed mark
> That looks on tempests and is never shaken;

the innocent loyalty of Desdemona, the generosity of Hermione and Cordelia in their forgiving love, the sturdy faith and loyalty of Paulina remain something of unrealized ideals in our work-a-day world, saving a few saints.

Shakespeare might have begun the Beauteous Youth Sonnets in a Platonic spirit of looking at love philosophically and in a disinterested enjoyment of the young man's physical beauty as an artist enjoys himself with the beauty of his model. The exhortation to marry and beget copies of his beauteous self comes naturally. Gradually, the ambiguity of love begins to make itself felt in the relationship. Love depends on beauty for its awakening; hence, is dependent for its continuance on the stability of beauty. Secondly, love seeks to possess. It must be reciprocated with love. Otherwise, it sulks and suffers and infects the very air with complaint. For the poet, sight of beauty satisfies hunger in love. And the perpetuity of this sight is all that is demanded. On the second plane we may interpret Venus as love seeking desperately for an expression through love made whole by reciprocating love from Adonis. At this point the Beauteous Youth resembles Adonis in his coldness towards love, turning waywardly against the warning of the poet to "hunt the bear"—the killer of beauty.

> How sweet and lovely dost thou make the shame
> Which like a canker in the fragrant rose
> Doth spot the beauty of thy budding name!
> Oh, in what sweets dost thou thy sins enclose!
>
> (*Sonnet 95*)

> Lilies that fester smell far worse than weeds.
>
> (*Sonnet 94*)

How amazingly does nature provide commentary on human life! Ultimately we find the poet and the Youth like a drowning man and his rescuer in the flood, rationalizing their situation as best they can:

So shall I live supposing that thou art true
Like a deceived husband; so love's face
May still seem love to me, though alter'd new—
Thy looks with me, thy heart in other place.

(*Sonnet 93*)

Another Sonnet bewails the loss of love in a manner that shows absolute loyalty, clearly implying that his life is inextricably united with the young man's:

When thou shalt be dispos'd to set me light,
And place my merit in the eye of scorn,
Upon thy side against myself I'll fight,
And prove thee virtuous, though thou art forsworn.

(*Sonnet 88*)

This feeling is echoed again and again in the plays:

It is my soul that calls upon my name.

(*Romeo & Juliet*, II.2.165)

Make me a willow cabin at your gate,
And call upon my soul within the house.

(*Twelfth Night* I.5.252)

There can be wide difference in interpretation of the *Sonnets* considered as a unity, as a growth, or as unrelated episodes. That is to consider Shakespeare as having a stable philosophy, or as searching for one, or without one. And as scholarship has not exhausted possibilities of fresh insight, it appears critically reasonable to build upon the Unitarian concept. Then only is it possible to bring one part of his work to bear upon another without constraint of chronological concern.

A third face of Love's ambiguity reveals itself in the poet's insistence on the independence of his love of external change, and its sufficiency to meet the forces of time. It is not the visible changes that time leaves in its wake which is now the greatest enemy of love, but the change of heart. G.F. Waller is not as convincing as usual to read the poet's assertion against Time in *Sonnet 116* as

> a deliberate and fearful repression, an unwillingness to acknowledge that Love is not able to overcome Time,[43]

suggesting that the poet is conscious of the failure even of Love to conquer Time. It is true that the poet acknowledges Time's supremacy over all that is mortal in love, including that love whose basic motive is utilitarian.

> If my dear love were but the child of state,
> It might for Fortune's bastard be unfather'd,
> As subject to Time's love or to Time's hate,
> Weeds among weeds, or flowers with flowers gather'd.
> No, it was builded far from accident;
> It suffers not in smiling pomp, nor falls
> Under the blow of thrilled discontent,
> Whereto th'inviting time our fashion calls.
> It fears not Policy, that heretic,
> Which works on leases of short-numb'red hours,
> But all alone stands hugely politic,
> That it not grows with heat nor drowns with show'rs.
> To this I witness call the fools of time,
> Which die for goodness, who have liv'd for crime.
>
> (*Sonnet 124*)

The testimony of Time and its power is overwhelming indeed, and love makes no compare in like strength:

> Since brass, nor stone, nor earth, nor boundless sea,
> But sad mortality o'ersways their power,
> How with this rage shall beauty held a plea,
> Whose action is no stronger than a flower?

The beauty of a flower is magnificent beyond imagination, and to think of its short lease in relation to "rocks impregnable" and "gates of steel" (even which time decays) is truly "fearful meditation." Love becomes a fugitive of Time, a jewel stolen from the lair of a dragon:

> Shall Time's best jewel from Time's chest lie hid?
> Or what strong hand can hold his swift foot back?
> Or who his spoil of beauty can forbid?

O, none, unless this miracle have might,
That in black ink my love may still shine bright.

(*Sonnet 65*)

Beauty fails, love fails to withstand death and separation, mere physical love leads but to hell. Still the poet asserts his love, though he knows that love too will die with him, unless a kind of transcendence is achieved.

But thy eternal summer shall not fade
Nor lose possession of that fair thou ow'st:
Nor shall Death brag thou wand'rest in his shade,
When in eternal lines to time thou grow'st.
So long as men can breathe or eyes can see,
So long lives this, and this gives life to thee.

(*Sonnet 18*)

Yet, do thy worst, old Time. Despite thy wrong,
My love shall in my verse ever live young.

(*Sonnet 19*)

First the poet brings the power of procreation against the power of Time. Now it is humble black ink that he brings to the van in his war against Time. What better immortality can be assured to things mortal than to live "so long as men can breathe"?

"The foundation of Shakespeare's comedy and tragedy", says Helen Gardner, "is the conception of man as finding his fulfillment in love, and therefore as not self-sufficient, but dependent upon others".[44] The Sonnets do not offer sufficient scope for a fuller and more diversified treatment of love, time and mutability as the plays have done. It is in the tragedies and the comedies that Shakespeare finally vindicates romantic love, (by which is understood the love between man and woman which is not dependent on, but does not renounce sexual relationship). The spirit of love in the plays, in fact, spreads its bright influence beyond the circle of lovers, sowing seeds of goodwill and forgiveness, establishing a new foundation of hope for a better society. The love of the poet of the *Sonnets* has triumphed over the power of Time not so much by constancy (which is subject to Time) as by finding a vehicle for his love which can race with Time. However, the love which is the preoccupation of the *Sonnets* has little or no sociological value, and is more or less of the nature of a young poet's exercise on popular theme and convention, though by this it is not at all implied that the poet's feelings are imaginary and have no real base. What is suggested is that, apart from the richer treatment of love in the plays, the *Sonnets* by themselves provide sufficient basis for a comprehensive view of love. Neither do they provide adequate insight into the unique relationship between the opposite sexes which normal experience would expect them to corroborate. Instead, the *Sonnets* regard such love as too fraught with dangers, if not altogether destructive. The plays, however, seem to treat of love in a manner which is felt along the blood. The antithesis between the sensual and rational love is not resolved without the characters involved undergoing significant changes in their attitude to and opinion of others and the world and life at large. The stronger one asserts will and individualism the lesson to be learnt proves harder. There are a few characters who possess a kind of personality which enables them to respond without friction to the unkindness of Fortune; and they represent the ideal in flesh and blood of true love which *fallen* man is truly capable of in an uncompromising universe under the sovereignty of the silent gods—that is, in so far as man expects them to act.

The tenor of romantic love in Shakespeare's Comedies is love at first sight; and fulfils to some extent the Petrarchan masochistic love-pangs of unrequited love. So in *Love's Labour's Lost* the King and his lords found their resolutions powerless against the flaming arrows of female charms, and each felt the "bird-bolt under the left pap", inspiring him to write odes to his mistress's praise. Berowne denounces their former vows to studious celibacy as "flat treason 'gainst the kingly state of youth", and breaks into seventy lines of discourse on Love, which speaks for them all. His theme is

But love, first learned in a lady's eyes,
Lives not alone immured in the brain,
But with the motion of all elements
Courses as swift as thought in every power,
And gives to every power a double power,
Above their functions and their offices.
... ...
And when Love speaks, the voice of all the gods
Make heaven drowsy with the harmony.
Never durst poet touch a pen to write
Until his ink were temp'red with Love's sighs;
O, then his lines would ravish savage ears,
And plant in tyrants mild humility. (IV.3.323-45)

which inspiration he attributes to the charms of women, showering them with apotheosizing accolades:

They are the books, the arts, the academes,
That show, contain, and nourish, all the world.
(348-49)

This is of a different tune from the Ovidian treatment of "my mistress's eyes" in the *Sonnets*—

But at my mistress's eye Love's brand new fir'd,
The boy for trial needs would touch my breast.
(*Sonnet 153*)

Donne achieves a calm religiousness in

So must pure lovers soules descend
T'affections, and to faculties,
Which sense may reach and apprehend,
Else a great Prince in prison lies.
To'our bodies turne wee then, that so
Weake men on love reveal'd may looke;
Loves mysteries in soules doe grow,
But yet the body is his booke.
(*The Extasie*)

This is to look on "love revealed" as a matter-of-fact routine of any love worth the name, whereas Shakespeare's unquenchable moral instinct cannot but see the same situation as a surrender to inevitability:

> ...but I, my mistress' thrall,
> Came there for cure; and this but I prove:
> Love's fire heats water, water cools not love.
>
> (*Sonnet 154*)

In a comic irony, however, the objects of the heady passions of the King of Navarre and his lords, the French Princess and her ladies prove more rational than to trust the untutored victims of Cupid's darts, and put them on probation of twelve months' penance. And who can say that Love's labour is lost? But that's "too long for a play".

The real love's labour's lost is Romeo's pining love for Rosaline, or of Orsino's distraction for Olivia. In contrast to Berowne's

> Love's feeling is more soft and sensible
> Than are the tender horns of cockled snails,
>
> (IV.3.333)

Romeo's

> Is love a tender thing? It is too rough,
> Too rude, too boist'rous, and it pricks like thorn
>
> (I.4.25-26)

presents youthful love in the Ovidian mode. Such youthful melancholy love, of which Laertes warns Ophelia against Hamlet's approach, and which Duke Orsino indulges in, is the worse in comparison with the love which "feeds on the air", and makes Valentine forget dinner, lending Romeo "love's light wings" to "o'erperch" Capulet's high walls—he who even now has been unable "To soar with his light feathers...above dull woe". Proteus's love for Julia in *The Two Gentlemen of Verona* lacks the true spirit of Valentine's love which is capable of sacrificing his own happiness for his friend—which seems absurd to Emily Pearson.[45] After a due penitence for his mercenary concept of love which respects no friend, Proteus discovers that true love is not so much a matter of looks as it is a matter of mind:

> What is in Sylvia's face but I may spy
> More fresh in Julia's with a constant eye?
>
> (V.4.114-5)

thereby qualifying Julia's self-evaluation:

> What should it be that he respects in her
> But I can make respective in myself...?
>
> (IV.4.190)

Having seen the stuff that he is made of, and knowing the meaning his name 'Proteus' carries, it is only to be mentioned that Proteus does not give us the kind of true conviction of his reformation. It seems exactly by the same protean facility that he utters the words just quoted, and Julia's future happiness seems less assured than that of Silvia.

The cowardly courtship of Thurio who flatly refuses to "endanger his body for a girl that loves him not", while very sensible (perhaps more so than Aguecheek's decision to go home after despairing of Olivia's favour), puts us in mind of reckless risks taken by true lovers for the sake of love. True love, in Shakespeare, has a price which only love can pay. Julia, Imogen, Viola, Rosalind, every one of them women of good breeding, dons a boy's garb, sets out to solve her own problems without as much a prayer for supernatural intervention as the situation demands. Disguise, in fact, has significant dramatic effect apart from its service to exigency, inspiring a number of essays on the theme of appearance and reality.[46] But here disguise is a means to safeguard the chastity of the heroines, only by which the fidelity of their love is assured. The problem of feminine chastity as a symbol of truth in love recurs in Shakespeare more than once. Initially, *The Rape of Lucrece* (1594) deals with the self-condemnation of Lucrece for the 'forced stain' on her chastity. The fact that her mind is untainted with the rape does not undo her physical violation. What is of paramount significance in Lucrece's estimate of her misfortune is that she is incapable of divorcing the body from the mind—a dichotomy modern man has no difficulty in assuming. The same problem is treated in *Cymbeline* in which the main event is centred in the mind of the husband while the wife is saved the real dishonour. Shakespeare's art of dramatizing 'real' events psychologically has matured considerably.

The course of love is not easy. Only a true lover may come unscathed through the flames of love's altar. No sacrifice less than self-hood appeases the god of love. Consciously or unconsciously, a lover in Shakespeare braves dangers and eventualities to the extent of recklessness or self-abandon. Romeo has some uneasy foreboding of danger; yet it does not deter him in his progress towards love:

> ...my mind misgives
> Some consequence, yet hanging in the stars,
> Shall bitterly begin his fearful date
> With this night's revels and expire the term
> Of a despised life clos'd in my breast,
> By some vile forfeit of untimely death.
> But he that hath the steerage of my course
> Direct my sail!
>
> (I.4.106-13)

Recklessness and faith combined, indeed! The rest of the story is about love bargained with danger and death.

The wild country of Wales is no Arden for Imogen. But she does not count the dangers, but the love of her banished husband who is not coming but has ordered her 'execution' for alleged infidelity. And the name she has assumed in the boy's shape is, ironically, Fidele. One is struck by the severity of lovers' punishment for infidelity in Shakespeare, which is usually no less than the removal of the offending individual from existence altogether, without a trace, if possible. The world is too good for such who trample on holy love.

For Viola, disguise is a means not merely for safety, but to stay within the bounds of civilized order, which alone can provide the survival she needs as a virtuous woman of noble birth. Her own brother vouchsafes that "she bore a mind that envy could not but call fair", accounting her beautiful in other people's eyes. Her mental maturity revealed in extreme situation is indicative of her good breeding. Her parentage has to be kept secret till such time as due recognition and restitution are assured. Before that her situation is desperate, and she knows that exposure to the world in her true identity may even endanger her life. Self-confident and self-provident, she possesses a strong faith where her quick brain and her situation are at their wits' end. Then her text is,

> What else may hap, to time I will commit. (I.3.60)

And she can really let go, and trust providence. Lear almost achieves this when he finds that self-pity of thinking on his daughters' unkindness was robbing him of his reason:

> O, that way madness lies; let me shun that.
>
> (III.3.21)

Viola discovers that her efficiency as the Duke's love-bearer has ended up in a closed triangle of unrequitting love, which only the appearance of Sebastian as the complementing alter ego of Viola's double role as lover and loved can open to make a double pair of mutual lovers. In an interesting development of Shakespeare's attitude to Time and Mutability, *Twelfth Night* depends on time for the solution of the problems of life and of love. This is a significant departure from the typical attitude of hostility towards Time that we have seen in the Sonnets and some of the plays. This shows that Time is felt in exact relation to its effect on a person's life. St. Augustine tried to understand the mystery of time, seeing it as a subjective concept, and "is in the human mind."[47] Rosalind in *As You Like It* says as much:

> Time travels in divers paces with divers persons.
>
> (III.2.302)

Lovers' time is measured by the sighs and groans. It is too lazy-footed to bring lovers to their happiness; but too swift-footed to depart when that is got. Juliet chafes at her Nurse's delay in bringing news from Romeo about their marriage:

> Love's heralds should be thoughts
> Which ten times faster glides than the sun's beams
> Driving back shadows over lowering hills.
>
> (II.5.4-6)

She chides the "fiery-footed steeds" of Phoebus for their unhurry in her haste for "gentle night" to give her her Romeo. But the events that fill Time between her expectation and her consummation makes the morning lark sing too soon! The sense of Time's betrayal of love in this play is overpowering: the happiness of the too too young lovers seems like theft of a jewel from the womb of Time.

Paradoxically, Proteus, notwithstanding the immaturity of his love for Julia, has shown his love as dependent on time and thus doomed to extinction;

> O, how this spring of love resembleth
> The uncertain glory of an April day,
> Which now shows all the beauty of the sun,
> And by and by a cloud takes all away!
>
> (2 Gent. of Ver. I.3.84-87)

The heat, while it lasts, may have equal intensity with Julia's love for him; yet the difference is measured by the standard of *Sonnet 116*, whose constant and enduring quality judges Proteus's love as 'Guilty', whereas Julia's love deserves highest honour for being constant against inconstancy, and bearing "it out even to the edge of doom".

Psychological studies of love and the power of loving throw favourable light on Shakespeare's treatment of love in his later plays. Psychologically healthy persons or "self-actualized" persons

> have a heightened appreciation for life, others and themselves, a detachment from the conforming aspects of culture, and an originality or creativity that ranks them far above the level of their fellows.
>
> They possess a quality that may be called 'humility' of a certain type while they are well aware of their own worth, there is no humbleness of the cringing or designing type.[48]

Against the conventional view of love as a deficit need, an emptiness which has to be filled, Abraham H. Maslow holds the view that psychologically healthy persons need less love than they can give to others. According to him,

> self-actualized persons tend toward an increasing spontaneity, resulting in the dropping of pretenses, roles and strivings in the love relationship. In such a union, it is not necessary to impress, suppress or repress. They can be themselves without feeling there are demands or expectations placed upon them. Such persons usually possess the ability to love and to be loved.... Such people do not need sensuality, but they enjoy it wholeheartedly...erotic and agapean love merge in the healthiest people. While in the general public, they appear to be at opposite poles, in self-actualized people the dichotomies are resolved; they are at the same time selfish and unselfish, active and passive, masculine and feminine, etc.
>
> These "self-actualized persons experience 'need identification'; they feel others' needs as if they were their own... their love is a spontaneous admiration, a sort of receptive and undemanding awe and enjoyment such as that experienced when one is 'struck' by a fine painting.[49]

There can hardly be another psycho-analysis of Shakespeare's lovers which comes nearer the actual than this. Shelley, too, has identified love as

> a going out of our own nature, and an identification of ourselves with the beautiful which exists in thought, action or person, not our own.[50]

But Keats has supplied the link of sympathy between nineteenth-century Romantic spirit and the Shakespearean synthesis of mind and body, ideal and mundane, dream and reality by realizing the need to participate in the actual conditions of human life if the ideal of beauty were to be achieved. Graham Hough has rendered concisely the Keatsian synthesis by which Shakespeare's ideal of love is thrown in relief:

> the attempt to reconcile the loveliness of the world with its transience, its pleasures within its pain, the longing to enjoy the beautiful with the suspicion that it

> cannot be long enjoyed unless much that is not beautiful is faced.[51]

And Keats has observed this faculty operating almost as second nature in a number of Shakespeare's characters. Perhaps it is this revelation of human sympathy that Keats has identified in Shakespeare as *Negative Capability*: not just an artistic detachment but a deep-rooted feeling of unity with the rest of creation, which may not be unlike what we see in Donne when he says,

> Any man's *death* diminishes *me*, because I am inuolued in Mankinde.[52]

It is impossible for a reader of Shakespeare who possessed a normal degree of human sympathy not to appreciate the feeling of confidence and security as well as the innate will to good towards others exuding from the 'good' characters in his plays. Truly, Shakespeare's concept of Love in its final development transcends both the Platonic cult of Beauty and the depressing consciousness of Time's tyranny. Ultimately, it does not seem to matter whether man finds a way to beat Time, or whether he has found a way to arrest mutability. Shakespeare has opened the book of human nature for us to see our situation in respect of space-time existence and the timeless internal world of consciousness.

> He has made everything beautiful in its time. He has also set eternity in the hearts of man.
>
> (*Ecclesiastes* 3:11)

He brings to us the only possible choice of existence, not in spite of the ruthlessness of indomitable forces beyond our power to control, but on the condition of a duty to perform. Portia of Belmont and Viola of Messaline have made the wise choice in building a candle light of love's world to shine in 'a naughty world'. The Biblical injunction that "it is more blessed to give than to receive"[53] is the underlying principle of the Love which brightens the world darkened, like Venice, by the Shylocks, the Iagos, the Angelos, the Malvolios, and the darkest of them who give opportunity to these enemies of love: Time and its attendant Mutability.

How far that little candle throws his beams!
So shines a good deed in a naughty world.

(*The Merchant of Venice,* V.1.90)

It is just a candle light, but it is enough to show what Love is, and what it is capable of achieving in the transformation of life. So shines Antonio's many good deeds in Venice. His hard anti-Semitism quite out of tune with his gentle bearing does not mar the light of his self-sacrificing love.

> Greater love hath no man than this, that a man lay down his own life for his friends.

(*Holy Bible:* St. John 15:13)

Against the actuality of Antonio's sufferings for the happiness of his friend Bassanio's protestation of his willingness to lose all for love seems called for by the need of the situation, and does not convince as strongly; seeing it comes from one who has just now desired the judge to

Wrest once the law to your authority;
To do a great right do a little wrong,
And curb this cruel devil of his will.

(IV.1.210f)

Love should be 'made of sterner stuff', the stuff that would rather not possess than possess at the loss of virtue, the very essence of love. Without the sanctity of virtue love becomes a mere object of Venetian bargaining. The place of virtue in love is therefore not equated with maidenhead, but it is in the heart. Love as the capacity to give and to forgive, to receive graciously, even to lose magnanimously where no gratitude is coming, is the subject of John Russel Brown's study of *The Merchant of Venice*—Love's Wealth and Judgement of *The Merchant of Venice.*[54] The rich glitter of Venice has its appropriate image of wealth to illustrate the essential philanthropic nature of love. The only exception to Antonio's grace—his hatred of Shylock and his unbiblical usury—is quite legitimate in the contemporary Christian revulsion against the tribe of Judas. Caricaturing the lucrative propensity of Jews seems to be an Elizabethan dramatic stock-in-trade.

Shakespeare, however, shows his greater sympathy for the common human spirit (not excluding a Jew) by portraying Shylock as the victim of historical aberration of Christianity. In that context Antonio would have been merely unchristian had he been less vindictive: as if he did not take part in the divine displeasure against the race which rejected the Messiah. On the other hand, Antonio's ordeal might not have been altogether undeserved. Religious dogmatism apart, it is no gentlemanly action to spit on a person, to spurn and call him dog. What Antonio had done to Shylock and is doing and says he will do amount to a *hubris* which turns the 'whirligig of time' with its revenges primed and timed.

The usury of the lovers, on the other hand, is of the giving kind. Antonio "lends out money *gratis* and brings down/ The rate of usance here with us in Venice," says Shylock. The law of grace and the law of usury are mutually opposed to each other. When Antonio outsteps his rule of grace and borrows after the law of Shylock's usury, he must necessarily pay according to the interest laid down in the reckless bond. And no law but mercy alone can deliver him from the forfeit of that bond he has signed in superfluous confidence on fickle fortune. Portia despaired of mercy and allows the law to take its course, and by the law is Shylock beaten at his own game. Any other judge, even the real Bellario, could never have seen the flaw in the bond, but Portia whose sense of justice and truth is never altered by her personal interest in the case. She has been faithful to her father's will, and in the court would rather lose the case and her husband's happiness in allowing the law declare Antonio guilty than save him by "wresting" the law from its true bent. It is the story of Abraham's sacrifice of his son Isaac all over again: the gift of the ram as Isaac's substitute is repeated in the discovery of the flaw in the bond as a reward for faith and integrity. "But seek ye first the kingdom of God, and His righteousness; and all these things shall be added unto you"[55] cannot be fulfilled more honourably. In Shakespeare, love is given freely, often entailing the need to let go of the very happiness strived for. This is not just a sort of some metaphysical certainty, but the very essence which makes love so valuable that it becomes a power. The suspense of Portia's waiting for Bassanio making his choice of the caskets and the possibility of losing him by a margin is so real that the exuberance of her joy at his choosing rightly comes as a sudden release of pent-up tension of fear and foreboding of love's doom. Her joy is no less than the joy Romeo would have felt had he come a minute later at the tomb. It is the joy of a resurrection. Love has been born, but now its stay and increase with time is assured.

In Shakespeare's Romances, we find implicit in the unfailing reward of self-sacrificing love and unconditional forgiveness and repentance the existence of intrinsic moral order in the collective conscience of humanity. The gods who refuse to intervene make their will perceived in the infinite will of man goodness even in things evil, provided that man would care enough to seek it with all his heart. This is what Duke Senior in *As You Like It* has come to learn in the Forest of Arden.

> Sweet are the uses of adversity;
> Which, like the toad, ugly and venomous,
> Wears yet a precious jewel in his head;
> And this our life, exempt from public haunt,
> Finds tongues in trees, books in the running brooks,
> Sermons in stones, and good in everything.
>
> (II.1.12-17)

For a humanist, this constitutes salvation—salvation from external circumstances, salvation from self.

And thus the pageant of Shakespeare's insubstantial world objectifies for us our essential humanity which our conventionality and drudgery often do not allow us to see. We are so very often prevented from living our lives alone to discover the stuff we are made of. We hide behind the façade of society, and sit safe in its accumulated strength like the old builders of Babel, ignorant of our innate strength. Shakespeare turns the facets of our intellectual and emotional being against the light of an impartial reason as only a 'chameleon poet' can do without taking part in the drama, and yet not insensitive to it. Does it really make a difference to put Shakespeare's portrayal of love beside that of St. Paul's, so long as the affinity between the two are evident and their theses capable of being realized on this side of the grave, though "the rest is," as yet, "silence"?

Time and the shifts it brings are relevant only so long as man considers externals which are subject to time, like physical beauty and love which feeds on "nature's rarities". As long as the Poet in the Sonnets bases his love on the physical beauty of his Friend it is inevitable that his love suffers continual fears:

> For never-resting time leads summer on
> To hideous winter and confounds him there;
>
> (*Sonnet 5*)

so that,

> Thy end is truth's and beauty's doom and date.
>
> (*Sonnet 14*)

Physical beauty lives on by generation only,

> And nothing 'gainst Time's scythe can make defence
> Safe breed to brave him when he takes thee hence.
>
> (*Sonnet 12*)

It is therefore in spite of Time's toll on external beauty that the Poet in *Sonnet 108* asserts the unaided constancy of his 'eternal' love,

> So that eternal love in love's fresh case
> Weighs not the dust and injury of age,
> Nor gives to necessary wrinkles place,
> But makes antiquity for aye his page;
> Finding the first conceit of love there bred
> Where time and outward form would show it dead.

With this 'internalization' of love where Time cannot touch and is forgotten, the Poet can finally celebrate in *Sonnet 116* the true essence of Love which does not depend on the external food of love:

> Let me not to the Marriage of true minds
> Admit impediments. Love is not love
> Which alters when it alteration finds,

Or bends with the remover to remove.
O, no! It is an ever-fixed mark,
That looks on tempests and is never shaken;
It is the star to every wand'ring bark,
Whose worth's unknown, although his height be taken.
Love's not Time's fool, though rosy lips and cheeks
Within his bending sickle's compass come;
Love alters not with his brief hours and weeks,
But bears it out even to the edge of doom.
If this be error, and upon me prov'd,
I never writ, nor no man ever lov'd.

And it is on the basis of this 'eternal' (in the sense, not of duration, but of absence or unconsciousness of time) nature of his love that the Poet in *Sonnet 123* challenges Time:

No, Time, thou shalt not boast that I do change.
Thy pyramids built up with newer might
To me are nothing novel, nothing strange;
They are but dressings of a former sight.

Time's permanence is by continual renewal and recycling; nothing is new, history repeats itself, finding fault with the past, not content with the present, the future unguaranteed. But "Love alters not" with time, and working with it, endures "even to the edge of doom", whatever that is.

Whether the end is a physical death only by which 'star-crossed lovers' find the union they desire, or the assurance of a new regenerated love born of severe trials, the plays of Shakespeare express in unison the power of Love to mould the entire intellectual and emotional framework of man. Time and Mutability, which overshadow the literary landscape of Elizabethan England, not excluding the works of Shakespeare, come to assume a more relative aspect with the growth of Shakespeare's dramatic imagination. There is no victory over Time in the sense of direct conquest and defeat; love does not make man immortal any more than any man has been killed by it. Neither can lovers kill with frowns any more than resurrect the dead with love. Time rolls Lucy in the diurnal course of nature; golden lads and golden girls come to dust for no fault of their own; and all must consign to elemental essence in their due time. Marcus Aurelius had taught harmony with time:

> Life in harmony with the universe is what is good; and harmony with the universe is the same thing as obedience to the will of God.[56]

Time, according to St. Augustine, is subjective; a mode of human response to change. He identifies three times:

> a present of things past, a present of things present, and a present of things future,[57]

that is, memory, sight, and expectation. The relativity of time in Shakespeare's plays, too, derives from the individual response to time in a given situation. T.S. Eliot relates time to human consciousness:

> Time past and time future
> Allow but a little consciousness.
> To be conscious is not to be in time.[58]

And Love is a consciousness. First of a need to be made whole by addition of and union with another; secondly of the need to make another whole and happy. Time and duration are measured in terms of the presence of this consciousness. The lark and the nightingale mutually change identities in relation to the lovers' changing consciousness of love and the intrusion of time in *Romeo and Juliet.*

In his essay, *King Lear and the great Tragedies,*[59] L.C. Knight places the conflict between the two time-worlds of the public world and the world of intense subjective experience in a question, asking whether the consciousness of love as a higher value has any tenability in the context of Time and Mutability. The Antony-Cleopatra relationship, so much subject to and so allergic to the necessity of living double lives, has no authentic reality until the moment of death, and the necessity of it to validate it.

> Morally there is not much to choose between Rome and Egypt; in matters of the heart and of the imagination, however, they are polar opposites.[60]

It is only when their dreams of power and glory have been trodden down into the dust that Antony and Cleopatra find their love for each other strong enough to endure the limit of human despair. They are, as it were, driven towards the warm embrace of the 'mutual flame' of their love. Notwithstanding the rather moralistic opposition of the values of love and duty, S.L. Bethel's essay on Antony and Cleopatra treats the last scene of the play with an uncommon sensitivity:

> Earthly defeat is the providential instrument of eternal triumph; it comes undesired, but when it comes, is freely accepted, and so converted into a process of necessary cleansing.[61]

The strength to accept death, not in the Roman stoical principle of saving one's honour, but in the spirit of Faith in the power of love to transcend temporality, implies Faith in a transcendental order. And the operation of a temporal moral order is implied too in the willing suspension of action where no action avails and one is left with no alternative but to trust in time and mutability. Death has no more horror for the lovers as it is the only means by which absolute spiritual union can be attained. This is not an escapist attitude; but the way, the only way, to overcome the enemies of true love. And by death alone is love capable of immortality. And that is equivalent to, and is meaningless without, an assertion of another order of existence

> Where souls do couch on flowers.

The Phoenix and the Turtle cannot be but find union in the mutual flame of the spirit that must fly from hence. The transcendental love of Antony and Cleopatra does not negate the possibility of be-ing in a time-bound sober existence while still asserting the power of love to lift one above the tempests of life. But even the time-world of the tragedies is inimical to the growth of love because of the difference of values they entertain. The world of Antony and Cleopatra, with its martial and historical necessity, cannot accommodate a royal romance any more than the world of besieged Troy can consider the love of Troilus and Cressida.

> ...in a war-dominated world, love is seen only in terms of appetite, exploitation, disease or battle.[62]

The real tragedy of love is when it is found powerless to transcend the situation in which it is placed, as in *Troilus and Cressida*. But even the cruelest twist of fate by the hands of Time in the robbing of lovers' earthly happiness fails to yield a true tragic feeling for the fact that love is fulfilled, albeit like a star that is gone to another universe.

The world of *Macbeth* where Time becomes Ambition's captive has no place for love. Time for Macbeth becomes a commodity whose value may be calculated in terms of crowns and castles:

> And nothing is but what is not. (I.3.141)

By usurping Time Macbeth desecrates Nature and the entire story reads like a gory nightmarish tale of unnatural events. Macbeth's crime has the nature of original sin in that he is egged on by his wife who even desires herself 'unsexed' and filled with 'direst cruelty'. Love and its attributes of faith and forgiveness are not the elements of *Macbeth*, a fact ominously anticipated early in the play by Duncan's misplaced trust in Cawdor and the safety of Macbeth's castle. It is a world where even the innocence of a child becomes seasoned cynicism:

> Then the liars and swearers are fools; for there are liars and swearers enow to beat the honest men and hang up them. (IV.2.55)

Macbeth and Richard III would desire no heaven of justice but an extinction of their being; for they too, like Lear, had been stretched upon the 'rack of this tough world' without having learnt to bear the affliction of their consciences. Their deaths release the time for others to live on.

In the earlier plays, character seems to play a significant role in working out the destiny of people. In spite of apparently resigned dependence on the wheel of chance, the characters do move the wheel by their actions and when it comes full circle, each gets the fruit of what one sowed, and time may appear to be less of a living force rolling men and women in its cosmic mill. The humanist in Shakespeare has now asserted itself in the full face of the universe and whatever horror may be lurking in its inscrutable unfathomable depths. Though humanism is not a substitute for religion, its claim for the human spirit grows and decreases in inverse proportion to the claim of religious faith in an external moral order. It appears, however, that it is his weakness and not his strength that makes man seek salvation in himself: weakness in being unable to admit the truth of his nature. Faith and reliance on unseen forces is possible only when one clearly understands the alternative viewpoint; when he realizes that there is no alternative at all:

> If I should cast off this tattered coat,
> And go free into the mighty sky;
> If I should find nothing there
> But a vast blue,
> Echoless, ignorant—
> What then?[63]

There hardly is anything more poignant in literature than Lear's final realization that moral good in the person of Cordelia is not necessarily blessed above the forces of evil:

> Why should a dog, a horse, a rat have life,
> And thou no breath at all? Thou'lt come no more.
>
> (V.3.506)

Lear's heart cracks, sending an endless echo that reverberates through the hollow universe.

The final plays strike a note of fresh faith in life where the storms of human passions have left death and despair. It is the mature Shakespeare who has learnt how to unify tragedy and comedy as common ingredients of life. No wonder the final plays are named 'Tragi-Comedies'. The elements of tragedy are still potent, and human weaknesses still have repercussions in ways that bring truly tragic feelings. Man, without a redeeming quality, can still be lost. But as Sukanta Chaudhuri points out, there is more freedom for external forces to bring results:

> In the last plays, substantially more than in Shakespeare's earlier work, effects far exceed the cause or occur entirely without cause; coincidences,

> improbable in themselves, occur in still more improbable succession; and fantastic if not openly supernatural events provide crucial turning points in the action.
>
> The effect of this freer structure is to loosen the link between human action and human destiny. In *Lear, Macbeth*, and *Antony and Cleopatra*, man had found the motive force of his being within himself; it is now transferred back to an external necessity.[64]

Shakespeare equates Love with cosmic order in *Othello*, and it is the loss of Love as he thinks which destroys Othello's universe. The role of chastity as a guarantee of love cannot be over-emphasized in these last plays; for the entire drama seems to be erected on this bedrock in each of these plays.

These plays open on a world disrupted by certain abuses of love. *Pericles* opens on the unimaginable parody of love by father and daughter living in incest without serious moral compunction. In *The Winter's Tale* the incredible jealousy of Leontes brings a cruel winter into his domain. True love in *Cymbeline* suffers from the traditional concept of aristocratic marriage. And *The Tempest* is an inevitable sequel to past offence against brotherly love. Thus the underlying concern in these plays appears to be the fundamental need for love to rejuvenate a degenerate society. But love in these plays is not more crucial for the young lovers as builders of tomorrow than for the old whose present actions have the power to make or mar their children's world.

And since the actions in these plays usually involve two generations, the relevance of Time becomes more significant. Time has to act as the vital link between the two generations while the interval of waiting becomes a cold winter of brooding melancholia. Time seems to sleep, and no action appears significant. But when Time wakes up, it ushers in the light of love as a breath of life blows into a vault of dead souls, working towards a cathartic purification, a togetherness, understanding and forgiveness in the wider world. While lovers are swept into each other's arms, enmities and misunderstanding are dissolved, and Nature smiles again as it may do in a post-apocalyptic world of universal purification.

Unlike the other romances, *Pericles* presents the entire story of a noble Prince whose education in the school of Love begins from the most loathsome picture to the most divine experience accompanied by 'music from the spheres'. That being a noble, generous, virtuous and loving Prince does not necessarily mark him out as Fortune's favourite is evident; and there seems to be insufficient evidence that Pericles has any influence on the events which rain happiness on him in the end. His nearest counterpart in literature is Homer's *Ulysses*. The preservation of his wife and daughter as well as the latter's winsome virtues are more the work of independent forces than they are the consequences of Pericles's actions. And perhaps this is what Shakespeare wants us to see: that forces beyond human will operate in the space-time dimension in a way human beings can respond to according to individual attitudes. Though Pericles has no way of knowing and preparing himself for his providence, there are countless possibilities and might-have-beens by which he may miss the opportunity that leads him to the right port. But again, he could not be mistaken so long as his life becomes a pilgrimage of love for his wife and child. It is Love that impels him, and Diana, the goddess of chastity whom Marina invokes, who guides him by a vision, directing him away from a bloody course of revenge to the most happy reunion of triune lovers. What greater happiness can heaven give than this moment which flesh is inadequate to express!

> This, this! No more, you gods! your present kindness
> Makes my past miseries sports. You shall do well
> That on the touching of her lips I may
> Melt and no more be seen. (V.3.41-44)

The role of Time has been reversed from that of destroyer to preserver, from being the agent of Mutability to being the agent of regeneration. But this is all a matter of attitudes. Indeed, it is not Time that has changed, but the Man. Man has usurped the moral centre with the result that he becomes the prisoner of his own attitude. Now that "The moral centre has once more passed outside man",[65] he is once more free to dream and look towards the heavens in that spirit which another poet shares:

> Behold, we know not anything;
> I can but trust that good shall fall
> At last—far off—at last, to all,
> And every winter change to spring.[66]

It has been spring in Sicily with good Leontes as King till Polixenes overstayed his welcome. The jealousy of Leontes springs from his underestimation of Hermione's love, and his lack of faith in others. It is apparent how Leontes has less external motivation for being jealous than even Othello, which is an indication of an inherent disease in his love. For he seems to be already bored with his friend as indicated by his brevity and lack of enthusiasm at the very beginning of the play. His seems to be a temperament more suited to councils of war and state than the softer cadences of love and friendship by the way he shows his lack of generosity and his inability to tell friendship from love. Once he persuades himself of his wife's guilt, he goes about it like a thorough judge, and shows no mercy. His actions are so preposterous that his subjects see in it a disease of which he must be cured.

Indeed, it is a disease of ignorance about love, the remedy for which will be found only when Time is ready to administer it. It is significant how Shakespeare has managed to harness the power of time for creation of a new world over the wrecks of yesterday. While the old world lies sadly brooding on memories in penitence, Time prepares the remedy in obscure Bohemia. Time is still arbitrary and independent of the human will; otherwise, Leontes's repentance has been awarded forthwith. And Paulina has no way of knowing about the baby's survival, thereby showing Time's autocracy. And while, like Pericles, Leontes has sufficient opportunities that can lead him away from the path of lovers' reunion, it is Paulina's good advice which perhaps makes him stay in the path of Time's re-creation.

Love in this play has suffered serious trials with irremediable consequences. In Shakespeare, such severe trials are essential to the process of purification and refinement, and love shines all the more brightly when the sufferings and tortures are over. The death of Mamilius and Antigonus, though may be done without, give force to the need of regeneration. Time can still be cruel in its intransigence, and the sacrifice is dear.

Again, it must be noted that Love in Shakespeare is total and as intransigent as Time is. Loyalty, chastity, and sacrifice are not merely ideals, but the very forms and image of Love, without any of which, it becomes a monster that devours and wreck human society. The consequences of Leontes's failure to trust in Hermione's love results in his isolation, which is worse than the isolation felt by Pericles because of a biting conscience. In *Hamlet*, we find the prince-lover, disoriented as he is already by his mother's infidelity, further pushed towards insanity when his lady-love finds prudence stronger than her love. But here in the last romances, we find young lovers asserting their loyalty to love in spite of heavy odds. Florizel proves his love for Perdita, strong enough to abjure filial duty and an heirship to hazard all at the bottom of a ship and the mercy of nature. And in *Pericles*, we see the ill-placed Marina rejecting the 'love' of a governor, only to win him truly by her rejection of his lust. Indeed, there is an almost magical quality about her chastity which gives her so much strength that she can almost dispense with our pity for her helplessness. It is a creed, a religion, a life-force with her, and she seems to exude certain divinity that marks her out as a moral and a spiritual votary. She therefore is not altogether helpless as Cressida in the Greek camp is. Others like Viola and Imogen do not feel so safe in their femininity as Marina, having to put on men's clothes. So too Rosalind. This is not to imply that Marina has certain immunity from the cruelty and vice of others; but that her chastity gives her a kind of protective shield which freezes the passion of her would-be molesters.

Chastity becomes a symbol of moral strength with Shakespeare, and the essence of morality is faith in a more perfect order than is found in human society. Wilson Knight's "A strong faith tends to render tragedy impossible," finds a base here. Faith in a meaningful order governing the systems may seem to explain the perseverance of Pericles and Leontes. The waiting and dependence on Time, the capacity to endure one's fate with a stoicism that will turn a Roman green with envy, indicates moral power. These new supermen and superwomen by their heroic assertions of the human will against external forces, more powerful than the inner forces warring against human ideals, have raised the level of tragic catharsis to a new height.

In *Cymbeline*, the moral thrust is on the theme of fidelity which Shakespeare has already studied earlier in *The Rape of Lucrece*—not fidelity in question, but one on trial. What makes the difference in the outcome of the story is that Imogen is a princess while the villain of the piece has more refinement than a Tarquin. And since the chastity of Imogen is not questioned, but confirmed, the emotional battle takes place in the heart of Posthumus. Imogen gets her share of heartache only when she reads her husband's letter to Pisanio wherein she finds herself wrongly abused. The scene of temptation is hardly interesting, knowing the stuff she is made of, except for the Iagovian art of Iachimo in lying. But the mainspring of the play's emotional force comes alive when Imogen braves the wild forests of Wales for love's sake in a mortal quest like a lamb going happily to the slaughter. The very inhumanity of the plot against her is appalling and unbelievable until we realize that Posthumous is as good a lover and a sucker as Othello. Donne seems to be more seasoned in love where Posthumus foolishly flouted his wife's virtue.

> If, as I have, you also doe
> Vertue'attir'd in woman see,
> And dare love that, and say so too,
> And forget the Hee and Shee;
>
> And if this love, though placed so,
> From prophane men you hide,
> Which will no faith on this bestow,
> Or, if they doe, deride:
> Then you have done a braver thing
> Then all the worthies did;
> And a braver thence will spring,

Which is, to keepe that hid.

(*The Undertaking*)

Posthumus makes trial of her love, but in reality, it is he whose faith in his love is being tried, and is found too weak and inadequate, while Imogen proves her borrowed name Fidele in all truth. And like Othello, Posthumus, after having recklessly exposed his wife to the libido of 'prophane' men, trampled madly on the carcass of his love, only to find that though he may kill her body, he cannot kill her inside himself where she lives. To have her living inside his soul, and know her to be dead is more than he can bear. But he loves more wisely than Othello in that he offers his life for a more meaningful sacrifice to what substance is left of her: her country.

But the most significant aspect of Imogen's love and her fidelity is again that mysterious power of grace and ethereal light she carries with her wherever she goes. Like Marina, she too seems to radiate sanctity when other women of her beauty would invite lust: Iachimo cannot bring himself to look on her with lust even in the bedroom. In fact, she seems to be a little cold in that kind of love in spite of her hot royal temper. Posthumus confesses that

Me of my lawful pleasure she restrain'd,
And pray'd me oft forbearance. (II.5.8)

When he learns from Pisano of her death by his command, he is guilt-stricken, though not yet resolved about her fidelity. He still loves her despite her alleged fault just as she loves him though her heart, "the innocent mansion" of her love is "empty of all things but grief", empty of the master

who was indeed/ The riches of it. (II.4.66)

Such strength in love, such persistence, such tenacity and long-suffering because of love, such generosity as cannot count blessing complete without forgiveness, making foes friends (that we find accompanying the love of Imogen and Posthumus) make the play another facet of the beautiful crystal ball with which Shakespeare makes his divination of human love.

Finally, *The Tempest* binds up the blessed vision of life-renewing Love in a manner which opens a new world for the regenerated people. Shakespeare has made liberal use of the supernatural in forging the minds and actions of his characters without suggesting any possible allegorical substitute for it in the powers within man's reach. Supernatural events are almost always external revelations of vital knowledge behind the veil of time and space inaccessible to man, yet which is dramatically essential to resolve the plot. But it is only in *The Tempest*, that a superhuman power is wielded by man at will, perhaps because Prospero's wisdom and maturity marks him out as a type of the Renaissance ideal of Man, who is identified by Tennyson as the type

> Of those that, eye to eye, shall look
> On knowledge; under whose command
> Is earth and Earth's, and in their hand
> Is Nature like an open book.[67]

Such is the god-like maturity of Prospero that his powers become more natural and beneficial than in Circe or Midas. And when he has done his god-like work of converting sinners, he is ready to cast off his "rough magic", the only substitute for which being 'prayer'

> Which pierces so that it assaults
> Mercy itself. (*Epilogue*)

The intriguing recapitulation of an earlier vision of universal flux and mutability in the hearing of two young lovers with promises of future happiness is so unexpected that Prospero even excuses himself for his "infirmity". It is the voice of Shakespeare in the Sonnets, and as accidental as it may appear, it forms the essential philosophical background of the new world that is under hectic preparation here in the island of nowhere.

Ours is an old world, and lots of things are being taken for granted, especially by younger ones. It becomes a birthright for every baby to grow up and inherit all that the parents have inherited, plus the best of present life. Life is full of promises when one looks up, but all is emptiness when one looks down.

Knowledge makes one 'old' and Prospero is doubly old, so that his vision embodies a seasoned knowledge of the essential nature of human life. It is a vision which, like a fairy tale to a child, sticks in memory to remind the young couples-to-be that Life is a miracle, "a dream-like projection"[68] of eternity, which must not be wasted but cherished and made fruitful.

However, love in *The Tempest* may look more like pre-planned, nurtured and overseen in contrast to the spontaneous and adventurous love of Florizel and Perdita. Yet, the love between Ferdinand and Miranda is not less true and spontaneous than that of Florizel and Perdita, or of Imogen and Posthumus, even if the circumstances are provided somewhat supernaturally. There is nothing wanting in it which does not become the usual ebullience of lovers' intoxication. Inspite of his apparent design to make his daughter 'Queen of Naples', Prospero has much ado to temper the effervescence of the love he has hatched from corroding the vessel which contain it.

> They are both in either's pow'rs; but this swift business
> I must uneasy make, less too light winning
> Makes the prize more light. (I.2.450)

And when he pretends to play the tyrant, he finds more opposition from Miranda, who tries to hold his arms from wielding the magic wand. A very significant action or inaction of Ferdinand succumbing to superior power throws light on the power of love to overcome that martial pride of man which makes Caesar almost a slave to it:

> Might I but through my prison once a day
> Behold this maid. All corners else o'th'earth
> Let liberty make use of; space enough
> Have I in such a prison. (I.2.490-93)

Yet, such joy of love needs to be qualified by a proper awareness of life's reality. Thus, when Miranda exclaims wonder-struck:

> How beauteous mankind is! O brave new world
> That has such people in't!

her father cuts her short in the same breath:

> 'Tis new to thee. (V.1.184)

He knows what she will find, where she is going, and for him, there is no idealizing about man. And that is why he is so careful of the lives of these two who are the promise of a new world.

A new awareness of time and mutability is expressed by the old Gonzalo, which speaks for the attitude of a number of other Shakespearean characters:

> Was Milan thrust from Milan, that his issue
> Should become King of Naples? (V.1.205)

Strange are the ways of Providence indeed! And it is a chastened group of people who are returning to an old world but with new minds and new hearts.

We have seen the progress of Shakespeare's treatment of Love as the essence of humanity, by which alone is the effect of time and mutability on life ameliorated and neutralized or even discovered to be of advantage. From a nagging sense of time as the number one enemy of human ideals and achievements through a horrifying vision of near despair in value-systems to a "wise passiveness, a ready adaptation to circumstances rather than a desire to control them",[69] Shakespeare follows the light of love, showing it as a divine power placed at the disposal of man. He has examined, with uncanny insight and god-like understanding, the secret depths of human personality, its strengths and weaknesses, and seems to have discovered that nothing short of love on a universal scale is going to answer the Renaissance call for human transcendence of exigent situations. So altruistic is Shakespeare's idea of love that even when he is treating love in the context of man and woman, we seldom find the usual 'romantic' attitude, but it is invariably substituted by a more social courtship by 'wit' and intellectual accomplishment.

Throughout his entire work Shakespeare never seems to let go of his concern for life and society. He sees these two as mutually interdependent for their survival. Love is the essence of the human spirit which controls the entire personality, supplying the energy for dauntless courage to face overwhelming odds. Keats speaks of the world as "a vale of Soul-making",[70] meaning thereby that true soul-hood is to be achieved by consciously opposing the resources of the spirit to the challenge of time and circumstances. And it is comforting to know that, behind the threatening voices of invisible forces

> There's a divinity that shapes our ends,
>
> Rough-hew them how we will. (*Hamlet*,V.2.10)

Even love itself falters and rots without this vision of an open moral system. *Othello* and *Macbeth* operate on a closed moral system where man seeks end in himself. Once the earthly vision evaporates, there is nothing to sustain the heroes but 'chaos'. Pericles leaves his world open, so that he is ready to receive at the hands of Providence a just reward for his patience, seasoned with 'Music from the Spheares'.

NOTES

1. E.D. Jones, *English Critical Essays—Nineteenth Century,* OUP, London, 1971, p. 78 the essay 'The Canterbury Pilgrims' by William Blake.
2. Andrew Lang, *The Approach to Shakespeare*, Thomas Nelson (UBS, Delhi 1969), p. 9.
3. 'Letter to Richard Woodhouse, October 27, 1818.' OAEL, p. 777.
4. *Keats, A Reading of His Major Poems*, Reliance, New Delhi, 1992, p. 5.
5. G.K. Hunter, *Humanism and Courtship*, Alpers, ed., *op. cit.*, p. 14.
6. Cf., L.G. Salingar, *The Elizabethan Literary Renaissance*: *Pelican Guide to English Literature*, ed., Boris Ford, Vol. 2, p. 53.
7. 'Measure for Measure', in *Shakespeare Criticism*, *1935-60*, ed. Ann Ridler, p. 2.
8. *Hamlet*, 2.2.248.
9. *Infirm Glory*, p. 154.
10. T.S. Eliot, 'Human kind/Cannot bear very much reality', *Four Quartets, Burnt Norton.*
11. M. Alexander, *op. cit.*, p. 214.
12. G. Wilson Knight, Ref. Endnote 2 of Introduction.
13. Harry Blamires, *A History of Literary Criticism*, Macmillan, 1991, p. 178.
14. Shakespeare and the Stoicism of Seneca.
15. The Holy Bible, 1 Corinthians, 13:8, 13.

16. Ivor Brown, *op. cit.*, p. 214: "...human sharks ravening at large among the small fish of the community."
17. *The Prince*, tr. George Bull, Penguin, 1977, p. 67.
18. Cf. Derek Traversi, *Shakespeare: The Young Dramatist*, Pelican Guide, Vol. 2, p. 179.
19. Alpers (ed.), *op. cit.*, pp. 236-37.
20. *Shakespeare's Sonnets*, George Allen & Unwin, 1982, p. 84.
21. Expostulation and Reply.
22. William Blake, *Auguries of Innocence.*
23. Matthew 6:21.
24. *Op. cit.*, p. 198-99.
25. *The Oxford Book of Literary Anecdotes*, Futura, London, 1977, p. 13.
26. Cf., C.F. Williamson, 'Themes and Patterns in Shakespeare's Sonnets', (1976), in *Shakespeare: The Sonnets*, A Casebook, ed. Peter Jones, Macmillan, 1977, p. 246; Muir, *op. cit.*, p. 85; and Waller, *op. cit.*, p. 234.
27. Pearson, *op. cit.*, pp. 284-85.
28. *Reason and Love in Shakespeare*, Triveni (1977), Machilipatnam.
29. *Ibid.*, p. 71.
30. *Ibid.*, p. 66.
31. *Shakespeare's Division of Experience*, Summit Books, New York, 1981.
32. *Ibid.*, pp. 21-22.
33. *Ibid.*, p. 22.
34. *Ibid.*, p. 24.
35. *Sacred Songs and Solos*, Marshall Morgan & Scott Ltd., No. 853.
36. Waller, *op. cit.*, pp. 227-28.
37. *Op. cit.*
38. *Op. cit.*, p. 102.
39. *War is Kind and Other Lines*, (1899), Sire, *op. cit.*, p. 13.
40. *Shakespeare Survey 15*, 1962, ed. A. Nicoll, p. 57.
41. Waller, *op. cit.*, p. 221.
42. Darling, *op. cit.*, p. 123.
43. Waller, *op. cit.*, p. 235.
44. *The Nobel Moor* in Anne Ridler (ed.), *op. cit.*, p. 369.
45. *op. cit.*, p. 288.
46. Richard Andretta, *Shakespeare's Romance*, Vikas, 1981 (Chapter 2: *Appearance and Reality*.)
47. Bertrand Russell, *A History Western Philosophy*, Simon & Schuster, NY, 1972, p. 354.
48. Darling, *op. cit.*, p. 89.

49. *Ibid.*, pp. 126-27.
50. A Defence of Poetry.
51. Graham Hough, *op. cit.*, pp. 162-70.
52. *Devotions upon Emergent Occasions*, ed., S.S.J. Elizabeth Savage, Salzburg, 1975, Vol. I, p. 122.
53. *Holy Bible*, Act 20:35.
54. *The Merchant of Venice*, A Casebook, ed. John Wilders, Macmillan, 1977, pp. 163-75.
55. *Holy Bible*, Matthew 6:33.
56. Bertrand Russell, *op. cit.*, p. 265.
57. *Ibid.*, p. 354.
58. 'Burnt Norton', *Four Quartets*.
59. *Pelican Guide*, Vol. 2, p. 247.
60. Robert Ornstein, 'The Ethic of the Imagination—Love and Art in Antony and Cleopatra', in *Shakespeare: Modern Essays in Criticism*, ed. Leonard F. Dean, Oxford, 1978, p. 395.
61. *Shakespeare and the Popular Dramatic Tradition*, London, 1944, pp. 116-31; also in *Twentieth Century Views: Shakespeare—The Tragedies*, ed. Alfred Harbage, Prentice-Hall, N.J., 1964, p. 166.
62. G.F. Waller, *The Strong Necessity of Time*, The Hague, 1976, p. 114.
63. Stephen Crane, *The Black Riders and Other Lines* (1895), from Sire, *op. cit.*, p. 76.
64. *Infirm Glory*, p. 193.
65. *Ibid.*, p. 197.
66. Tennyson, *In Memoriam*, Oxford Anthology, p. 1239.
67. *In Memoriam*, Epilogue.
68. Gauri Prasad Ghosh, 'The Mystery of Prospero's Vision', Part I of *The Insubstantial Pageant: A Study of the Development of Shakespeare's Life-Vision*, Orient Longman, 1970, p. 49.
69. *Infirm Glory*, p. 199.
70. *Letters to George, & Georgiana Keats, February 14-May 3, 1819*, Oxford Anthology, p. 782.

4

John Donne: Treatment of Love, Time and Mutability in his Poetry

Why love among the virtues is not knowne
Is, that love is them all contract in one.

John Donne—'To the Countesse of Huntingdon'

It may be true that the famous essay, *The Metaphysical Poets* by T.S. Eliot (1921) and H.J.C. Grierson's edition of Donne (1912) were responsible for a new enthusiasm over his poetry, which had been censored too rashly by Dr. Johnson. Yet another inducement can well be a certain affinity felt by our century with Donne and his Poetry. Such a view is advanced by Gary Waller:

> For many twentieth-century liberals, his poetry perhaps articulated some of their own aspirations: Donne was born into a persecuted minority, was a bold experimenter, a man who dared to face the emotional consequences of the 'new philosophy', and who explored in his poetry a refreshingly direct sexuality....[1]

The personality of Donne's poems, the 'I' whose experience makes up the world of these poems, speaks no less directly than the Poet of Shakespeare's sonnets. Perhaps more than Shakespeare, Donne has expressed, and not unlike Matthew Arnold—

wandering between two worlds, one dead,

The other powerless to be born—[2]

the spirit of the age, the strain of the withdrawing old world and its emotional stability, as well as a tremulous fear of the yet unfathomed new cosmos staring at him with a mindless impersonal gaze.

And new Philosophy calls all in doubt,
The element of fire is quite put out;
The sun is lost, and th'earth, and no mans wit
Can well direct him where to looke for it.

(The First Anniversary)

There is sufficient reference in his poems to lead some critics off course in presenting Donne's attitude to the two worlds, namely, the Ptolemaic world of ordered correspondences and the Copernican discovery of an open universe. It is true that Donne reacts significantly to the powerful current of ideas and shifts in philosophical speculations his age witnesses, and in a way which may be seen as a protest and a disillusioned cynicism. Yet, it should not be mistaken that Donne was revolted less by the 'decaying' old world than he was by the nature of decay which attends on mortality, and that the apprehension of the universal tendency to decay and annihilation was exacerbated—or thrown into kaleidoscopic relief—by the revolutionary world of ideas surrounding him. But it would not be consonant with any of his works, much less *The First Anniversary*, to suggest as Williamson has done, a Donne "suspended between two worlds, the old world of decay and the new world of Progress".[3] The fact that the 'new Philosophy' has made the old Philosophy irrelevant is not the theme of Donne's complaint. Rather, it is the breaking apart of a harmonious universe of the Elizabethan world picture by the new scientific speculations which has not then produced the correspondent unification of thought and feelings as the 'old' had done which rendered the poet's world so vulnerable to disillusion and cynicism. If the question were asked, which world Donne belongs to, the likely answer is that he belongs to the old one, for that is where his sensibility is more at home, if T.S. Eliot observes a 'dissociation of sensibility' in the later poets.

That it was a losing battle against the 'new Philosophy' is evident in the conscious bravado of *The Sunne Rising*, where, the newly enthroned usurper of the universe is made the butt of the poet's (and the lovers') sullen impatience. The bitterness of feelings wreaked against the 'unruly' Sun seems to erupt from a deeper sense of displeasure than mere annoyance at being prevented from having love's pleasure indefinitely. Lines such as,

> Must to thy motions lovers seasons run? (4)
>
> Thou sunn art halfe as happy as we,
> In that the world's contracted thus; (25, 26)
>
> Thine age askes ease, and since thy duties bee
> To warme the world, that's done in warming us.
> (27, 28)
>
> This bed thy centre is, these walls, thy spheare,
> (30)

in addition to an unwilling admission of the power of the sun to invade their microcosm, also slyly convey a petulant desire to hit back, to belittle a recognized champion, a stubborn refusal to be a passive hostage, and a chauvinistic assertion of man's indomitable spirit. Man has lost his place as the centre of the 'spheares', and with it all correspondence is gone too.

> Then, as mankinde, so is the worlds whole frame
> Quite out of joint. (*The First Anniversary*)

Murray Roston's assertion is still stronger. To him, *The Sunne Rising*

> constitutes a challenge to the New Philosophy itself, provocatively reaffirming in the face of all contrary scientific evidence the preeminence of man in the cosmic pattern, and the impregnability of his inner experience...the challenge emerges not as a mere braggadocio but as a reassertion of man's centrality in the universe, and above all [of] the inevitability of his inner being.[4]

And Sukanta Chaudhuri draws a humanistic conclusion:

> In the midst of a dissolving world-order, the accompanying fragmentation of knowledge, and the grossness, corruption and debility of man's estate, Donne asserts human power and dignity.[5]

Wherever such beautiful hero-making assertions may lead, there is always the danger of overstating the fact: the fact of the poet's purpose, which usually is the expression of an experience. And in Donne's case, this is more interestingly demonstrated in the light of T.S. Eliot's observation that Donne's sensibility was the sum of the fusion of his thought and feelings.[6]

The fact that Donne was concerned, not with the battle of ideas of his time, but with the effect of such environment upon his sensibilities, had been observed in the nineteenth century by Arthur Symons, who said that Donne

> was sincere to himself in expressing what he really felt under the burden of strong emotion and sharp sensation.... Donne is intent on the passion itself, the thought, the reality.[7]

Indeed, the Metaphysical Poets are identified, not so much by the way they employ intellectual conceits as by the way they feed real experience and thought to their intelligence. Theirs is not the idealist's sensation of a far-flung contemplation of a something just beyond the reach of mortality; they do not create a new world of poetry where the fancy may forget present pain. Theirs is the constantly self-conscious analytical vivisection of experience and attitudes which make the reading of their poems, especially those concerning sexual relationship, disquieting for the prudish. In fact, no one who has not achieved the fusion of mind and emotion, he who is incapable of coordinating thoughts and feelings, ideas and life, will ever understand Donne. The medieval concept of the body as more susceptible to evil than the spirit is totally alien to Donne's metaphysics. Just as in Keats we find the idea of Beauty and the sensations of concrete experience amalgamated to form a unified sensibility, so do we find Donne unifying gross flesh and ethereal essence:

So must pure lovers soules descend
T'affections, and to faculties,
Which sense may reach and apprehend,
Else a great Prince in prison lies. (*The Extasie*)

The degree of oneness experienced by the poet and his beloved transcends time and place, as well as individuality, which in itself is significant in the light of increasing individualism and self-centredness in congruence with the 'new Philosophy'. *A Valediction: forbidding mourning*, in that context, becomes particularly more poignant than if it had been a song of farewell:

As virtuous men passé mildly away,
And whisper to their soules to goe,
Whilst some of their sad friends doe say,
The breath goes now, and some say, no:

So let us melt, and make no noise,
No teare-floods, nor sigh-tempests move,
T'were prophanation of our joyes
To tell the layetie our love.

The simile of the conceit using the body and the soul as illustration of the lovers' union corresponds perfectly to that of the compass which are two yet one:

Our two soules therefore, which are one,
Though I must goe, endure not yet
A breach, but an expansion,
Like gold to ayery thinnesse beate.

If they be two, they are two so
As stiffe twin compasses are two,
Thy soule the fixt foot, makes no show
To move, but doth, if the'other doe.

And though it in the center sit,
Yet when the other far doth rome,
It leanes, and hearkens after it,
And grows erect, as that comes home.

Herein is the key to the canon of Donne's love poetry: namely, the sincere affirmation and demonstration of love and its power to unify the disparate experiences of body and mind. The concept of man's dual entity, which in the traditional Pauline sense assumes unity only after the body has been transformed into a finer essence, appears to be more at ease in Donne. Here the body and the spirit are not warring forces, but the two sides of a coin. And the question of eschatology does not arise in the poems dealing with love of woman wherein love is impossible without the body to make it an experience:

> Love must not be, but take a body too.
>
> (*Aire and Angels*)

Grierson sees "the suggestion of a new philosophy of love", which is less dualistic and ascetic than the Dantesque or Petrarchan concepts, in the poetry of Donne which is more fully informed by the poet's fullness of experience as a lover.[8] C.S. Lewis thinks of Donne as writing under the uncomfortable weight of the medieval sense of guilt about the sexual encounter.[9] These two apparently contrary views may combine to throw light on the nature of Donne's love poetry. For, either of these finds equal voice in the poems. *The Canonization* is particularly rich in such combination or fusion of apparently contrary images, called paradox:

> Call us what you will, wee are made such by love;
> Call her one, mee another flye,
> We'are Tapers too, and at our owne cost die,
> And wee in us finde the'Eagle and the Dove.
> The Phoenix riddle hath more wit
> By us, we two being one, are it.
> So to one neutrall thing both sexes fit,
> Wee dye and rise the same, and prove
> Mysterious by this love.

The language Donne uses, by its brevity and directness, helps to give his expressions, a certain lightness which can be mistaken for lightness and banter—a rakish lack of seriousness about the experience to make less serious readers believe that Donne is indulging in sexual abandon, that he takes love for fun. But Donne is quite serious about love, and about religion, as Cleanth Brooks points out.[10] Implied in Brooks's essay on this poem is that Donne cannot be more serious about the metaphor of the Phoenix and death and rebirth.

Unlike Petrarch and a number of other poets writing on love, "Donne never lets us forget the world outside the poem".[11] In fact, "the poem emerges as a speech out of the middle of a moving action, modified by its surroundings and referring spontaneously to them".[12] He knew very well the price he had to pay in terms of secular success as well as the danger to himself in pursuing the course of love. Indeed, the poem last quoted, perhaps more than any other poem, echoes with biographical spontaneity of feelings. His affair with Ann More and their subsequent deprivation by her irate father and his employer could well have triggered the staccato of fires in the first two stanzas. The quick salvoes of impatience and indignation effectively hammer in his determination to love against all odds:

> For Godsake hold your tongue, and let me love,
> Or chide my palsie, or my gout,
> My five gray haires, or ruin'd fortune flout,
> With wealth your state, your minde with Arts improve,
> Take you a course, get you a place,
> Observe his honour, or his grace,
> Or the Kings reall, or his stamped face
> Contemplate, what you will, approve,
> So you will let me love.
>
> Alas, alas, who's injur'd by my love?
> What merchants ships have my sighs drown'd?
> Who saies my teares have overflow'd his grounds?
> When did my colds a forward spring remove?
> When did the heats which my veines fill
> Add one more to the plaguie Bill?
> Soldiers finde warres, and Lawyers finde out still
> Litigious men, which quarrels move,
> Though she and I do love.

Brooks' lucid exposition of the poem sufficiently states the conflict between the 'real' world and the 'lovers' exclusive world of love. Others more materialistic in their attitude to love may scorn his impractical seriousness in love beyond the call of nature and convention. Later in life he himself looked back upon his "prophane love" with a holy fear, as in the *Holy Sonnets XIX*:

> Oh, to vex me, contraryes meet in one:
> Inconstancy unnaturally hath begot
> A constant habit; that when I would not
> I change in vowes, and in devotione.
> As humorous is my contritione
> As my prophane love, and as soone forgot:
> As ridlingly distemper'd, cold and hott,
> As praying, as mute; as infinite, as none.
> I durst not view heaven yesterday; and to day
> In prayers, and flattering speaches I court God:
> To morrow I quake with true feare of his rod.
> So my devout fitts come and go away
> Like a fantastique Ague: save that here
> Those are my best dayes, when I shake with feare.

Evidently, Donne swings like a pendulum from one extreme of unifying the spirit and the flesh in the act of love, to the other extreme of downright loathing and cynicism. Here Williamson may be right to say of Donne:

> But in all his contrarieties of mind he still wanted to make the most of both worlds.[13]

The two worlds refer to the old one of harmonious correspondences and the new one of dissociative individualism.

It is only the amazing range of Donne's introspection of his experience (remembering, of course, that, to Donne, 'thought' amounts to 'experience') which accounts for the apparently incompatible expressions of attitudes in love. Else it is difficult to believe that the poet of *The Good Morrow* and *Song: Goe and catche a falling starre* is the same person. We may consider such lines as the following against others of contrary sympathy in order to appreciate the full implication of the pressure Donne was put under:

> All other things, to their destruction draw,
> Only our love hath no decay;
> This, no to morrow hath, nor yesterday,
> Running it never runs from us away,
> But truly keepes his first, last, everlasting day.
>
> *(The Anniversarie)*

> O how feeble is mans power,
> That if good fortune fall,
> Cannot adde another houre,
> Nor a lost houre recall!
>
> *(Song: Sweetest love, I do not goe)*

In *Lovers infiniteness*, the poet tells his 'Deare' to ration out love to him so that he will have infinite love in reserve:

> Yet I would not have all yet,
> Hee that hath all can have no more,
> And since my love doth every day admit
> New growth, thou shouldst have new rewards in store.

But Love is not found in the possession of the beloved. Donne seems to confess in *Loves Alchemie*:

> Some that have deeper digg'd loves Myne then I,
> Say, where his centrique happiness doth lie:
> I have lov'd, and got, and told,
> But should I love, get, tell, till I were old,
> I should not finde that hidden mysterie;
> Oh, 'tis imposture all.

The deflation of expectation reminds us of Shakespeare's *Sonnet 129*:

> So, lovers dreame a rich and long delight,
> But get a winter-seeming summers night.

Joan Bennet categorically diagnosed the disparity, saying,

> Donne's poetry is not about the difference between marriage and adultery, but about the difference between love and lust.[14]

And that is where she appears to miss the mark in her attempt to discredit C.S. Lewis's view of Donne as unable to "get rid of a medieval sense of the sinfulness of sexuality for long." Her essay written as 'A Reply to Mr. C.S. Lewis' masterfully shows that Donne has elevated the sexual act to the level of pre-lapsarian innocence, but only so long as the "mysterie" of spirit-flesh unity is maintained. And the condition governing the possibility of the necessary transmutation is not easy to maintain. Lewis does not deny that Donne can get rid of the sense of guilt in the pre-marital or ex-marital sex as long as the power of his love can sustain it; but he denies that he can do it forever. And this is what frustrates the poet-lover: that love is dependent on sense and feelings which are punctuated by time, and thereby suffer change and death, "because love dies too."[15]

J.E.V. Crofts studies Donne against the backdrop of London in which the pageant of the aging Gloriana was

> paling under the light of an intellectual dawn, and her surviving knights and seneschals were revealed as a group of tired and pouchy-faced old men standing about the throne of a dreadfully painted old woman.[16]

His presentation of Donne as an angry poet of disillusionment hardly leaves anything to say of the lover whose beloved redeems all women, and whose element is the world's essence:

> Oh doe not die, for I shall hate
> All women so, when thou art gone,
> That thee I shall not celebrate,
> When I remember, thou wast one.
>
> But yet thou canst not die, I know;
> To leave this world behinde, is death,
> But when thou from this world wilt goe,
> The whole world vapors with thy breath.

But all this time, the poet never forgets that his mind is playing with a dream, that disease and death cannot be stayed even by the most exalted love:

> Yet t'was of my minde, seising thee:
> Though it in thee cannot persever.

For I had rather owner be
Of thee one houre, then all else ever. *(A Feaver)*

Crofts is dealing with the opposite swing of the pendulum when he writes,

> Love, when it comes, is not an experience which re-illuminates his life and wipes away the trivial, fond records of youthful apostasy. What we see is not the new man, the lover transfigured, but the coxcomb defeated: the man who in spite of all his cynical profession has gone and fallen in love after all. It is not love that inspires him so much as exasperation at feeling love.[17]

It is difficult to share the view that Donne, after all, rejects love both intellectually and passionately out of sheer cynicism, only to find himself no match for the power of love.

The problem, as Brooks has pointed out in *The Well-Wrought Urn*[18] appears to be the nature of the unity of lovers. To Donne mere Platonic love, however mysterious, is incomprehensible without the bodies sealing the union.

Wee then, who are this new soule, know,
Of what we are compos'd, and made,
For, th'Atomies of which we grow,
Are soules, whom no change can invade.
But alas, so long, so farre
Our bodies why doe we forbeare?
... ...
To'our bodies turn wee then, that so
Weake men on love reveal'd may looke;
Loves mysteries in soules doe grow,
But yet the body is his booke. *(The Extasie)*

This sense of unity can be carried to such a pitch that individuality dissolves into a new being which is neither the he nor the she, but each is the other's self. So in the tender *Song: Sweetest love I do not goe*:

When thou sigh'st, thou sigh'st not winde,
But sigh'st my soule away,

When thou weep'st, unkindly kinde,
My lifes blood doth decay.
It cannot bee
That thou lov'st mee, as thou say'st,
If in thine my life thou waste,
Thou art the best of me.

In their oneness the lovers build 'a world of their own', sustained by the equality of their love. Shakespeare has witnessed this union in *The Phoenix and the Turtle*:

So they lov'd as love in twain
Had the essence but in one;
Two distincts, division none:
Number there in love was slain.

But Donne knew that such "extasie" in love must be conditional. Thus in *The Good Morrow*:

What ever dyes, was not mixt equally;
If our two loves be one, or, thou and I
Love so alike, that none doe slacken, none can die.

The amatory pun on the word 'die' here assumes primary meaning; for Donne is not talking about death of the body, but of the death of love with the consummation of sex. The heaven of such love as depends on sexual orgasm as its end inevitably crumbles to become its own grave. This is what C. S. Lewis talks about, and Miss Bennet too: that Donne is troubled by the conflict of love and lust.

The paradox of love, therefore, is that loved must be felt along the nerves, but the experience of love in flesh results in an uncertain memory (for the mind can hardly recreate sensory experience), leaving,

A kinde of sorrowing dulnesse to the mind.

Easily, too soon, love becomes slave to the senses, depending on the sensual rapture of sex for its embodiment, only to be deluded of lasting satisfaction.

Ah cannot wee,
As well as Cocks and Lyons jocund be,
After such pleasures? *(Farewell to Love)*

To look for puns on the words 'Cocks' and 'Lyons', however, may stretch things too far; especially, when the sense is relatively satisfactory in the light of Redpath's reference to an idea from Galen that only cocks and lions possess priapean virility,[19] unless someone wants to stress the obsessive feeling of guilt after an illicit sexual encounter even before the sweeping flood of pleasure in lovers' bodies subside.

It becomes a crucial question as to how far Donne succeeds in his poetry in formulating a reliable philosophy of love. Miss Pearson's estimate of Donne as a passionate pilgrim whose sincerity and curiosity succeed in an unflinching revelation of the inadequacy of love to effect a stable unifying experience[20] in the bilateral relationship of man and woman offers a tangible rationale, without admitting defeat. Donne has not given up his search for the elixir which the possession of woman's body does not yield. And in the absence of any systematic dating of his poems except the great dividing line in his life when he, more out of necessity than choice, accepted ordination in the Church of England, the *Farewell to love* needs not be seen as a parting shot of the fox at the luscious grapes. The entire poem is not about love celebrated in *The Anniversarie*, *The Undertaking*, and *Song: Sweetest love, I do not goe*, but about what happens when love abdicates in favour of lust. This is why C.S. Lewis is particularly unhappy about Donne "drawing distinctions between spirit and flesh", seeing that, "the more he labours, the deeper 'Dun is in the mire', and.... *The Extasie* is a much nastier poem than the nineteenth Elegy." [21] Neither is this an admission of failure to find a satisfying experience in love; for a number of his poems testify that he did achieve a transcendental satisfaction to a degree beyond what 'a shudder in the loins' can possibly explain. As an example, the following couplet,

> Wee dye and rise the same, and prove
> Mysterious by this love *(The Canonization)*

contrasts the happiness of the perfect lovers immediately after having a physical consummation with the hollow experience of lovers who sought love in the physical union:

> the thing which lovers so
> Blindly admire, and with such worship wooe;
> Being had, enjoying it decayes:
> And thence,
> What before pleas'd them all, takes but one sense,
> And that so lamely, as it leaves behinde
> A kinde of sorrowing dulnesse to the minde.
>
> *(Farewell to Love)*

Evident in such antipathetic poem is the poet's close knowledge of the polarity of experiences, notwithstanding the gentlemanlike portrait of him by Sir Richard Baker as

> not dissolute, but very neat; a great Visiter of Ladies, a great frequenter of Playes, a great writer of conceited verses,[22]

To which H.J.C. Grierson has added colour:

> The blood was flowing passionately in his veins. He saw perhaps other sides of life in Italy and Spain than that of the Seminaries. He tasted of the sweets of Italian and Spanish poetry. He awoke to the allurements of pleasure and ambition and came home not at all disposed to become a missionary and a martyr as his brother might almost claim to have been, but more of the Inglese Italianato, not a debauchee like Robert Greene nor a defiant sceptic and enemy of Christianity like Marlowe, but a fashionable, brilliant young law student, avid of pleasure and of worldly advancement....[23]

The picture that emerges of Donne is that of an honest and passionate seeker of a wholesome synthesis of the total experience of love beyond the need of morals and convention to qualify its essence. To that end his love poetry is an experiment in as much as it is a revolt against and a flagrant disregard of convention and sobriety which appear hypocritical to him. Urmilla Khanna seems to have drawn too sharp a distinction between Shakespeare and Donne in regard to their moral feelings:

> Donne delights in the amoral pose that he assumes whereas the tormented lover of the Dark Lady is

> obsessed with the distinction between purity and corruption, truth and falsehood.[24]

For there are occasions when Donne could well have confessed with Shakespeare's *Sonnet 147*,

> My love is as a fever, longing still
> For that which nurseth the disease;
> Feeding on that which doth preserve the ill,
> Th' uncertain sickly appetite to please.

as in the verse letter *To the Countess of Huntington:*

> Yet since all love is fever, who to trees
> Doth talke, doth yet in loves cold ague freeze.
> 'Tis love, but, with such fatall weaknesse made,
> That it destroyes it selfe with its own shade.
> ... ...
> He much profanes whom violent heats do move
> To stile his wandring rage of passion, Love:
> Love that imparts in every thing delight,
> Is fain'd, which only tempts mans appetite.

Shakespeare's Platonic ideal suffers lamentable regress when the poet discovers Cupid's fire too strong in his mistress's charms that he must unwillingly rationalize the erotic impulse in such gross innuendos even Donne could hardly have written:

> Love is too young to know what conscience is;
> Yet who know not conscience is born of love?
> Then, gentle cheater, urge not my amiss,
> Lest guilty of my faults thy sweet self prove.
> For thou betraying me, I do betray
> My nobler part to my gross body that he may
> Triumph in love; flesh stays no further reason,
> But rising at thy name, doth point out thee
> As his triumphant prize. Proud of this pride,
> He is contented thy poor drudge to be,
> To stand in thy affairs, fall by thy side.
> No want of conscience hold it that I call
> Her 'love' for whose dear love I rise and fall.
>
> *(Sonnet 151)*

We do not have sufficient evidence to prove Shakespeare's illicit relations with other women. But it is impossible that his wife could be the "Dark Lady" of his Sonnets, to say which is to admit that there in all probability was a certain female. With Donne we have adequate reason to believe that his erotic fancy had the licence of a happy conjugal relationship which as implied below is jealously patented in a colonial metaphor— in *Going to Bed*:

> my kingdome, safeliest when with one man man'd.

Shakespeare plodded through the painful path of Love before discovering that

> Love is not love
>
> Which alters when it alteration finds.
>
> *(Sonnet 116)*

And if the love a woman can give through her body were the highest expression of Love, both Shakespeare and Donne concurrently refuse to compromise their ideal of love which they celebrate to the high degree of Petrarchan idolatry.

Thus, we should inevitably find Donne sardonical and cynical towards woman as a mere sexual object possessing no other virtues than the exterior beauty which allures men's love. *The Paradox*, *Loves Alchemie*, *Farewell to Love*, *Communitie*, *Song: Goe and Catche a falling starre* convey sufficiently strongly the disappointment and disillusionment of the poet in the false façade of love assumed by "moving beauties". 'Moving' here means 'which moves an appropriate response in the beholder'. But how easily even the irresistible feeling of being drawn as if by magic or as a moth to the flame, like Duke Orsino's 'appetite', 'sicken and die'!

> ...the thing which lovers so
> Blindly admire, and with such worship wooe;
> Being had, enjoying it decayes. (*Farewell to Love*)

Just as Shakespeare has rung "fancy's knell" in dismissal of courtly love in his Comedies,

> Tell me where is fancy bred,
> Or in the heart or in the head,

How begot, how nourished?
Reply, reply,
It is engend'red in the eyes,
With gazing fed; and fancy dies
In the cradle where it lies.

(*The Merchant of Venice,* I.3.63-69)

Donne too bids farewell to love which 'alters' every minute, and whose

....first minute, after noone, is night.

(A Lecture upon the Shadow)

A Lecture upon the Shadow finally relates the progress of love to time by means of the moving shadows lovers make as they walk in the sun. However, the sun and the time it tells are no more than metaphors of the sun of love and the change they embody in the progress of love.

Except our loves at this noone stay,
We shall new shadows make the other way.

Here it is not so much the sun that intrudes upon lovers' world as it is the sense, the premonition of love's inevitable decay: the fact of love's growth towards its climax being the fact of its decline too.

The morning shadowes weare away,
But these grow longer all the day,
But oh, loves day is short, if love decay.

Just as the hot noon begins the dying of bright day, the heat of love burns up the fuel of love, and

(...each such Act, they say,
Diminish the length of life a day). *(Farewell to Love)*

If, as Grierson thinks, the poetry of Donne has attained what he calls 'the true escape from courtly or ascetic idealism' in his treatment of love 'as a passion in which body and soul alike have their part, and of which there is no reason to repent',[25] on the basis of his love for his wife, the only way his poems could be understood is that of Donne rejecting the love that is 'grown all mind' and which grows all flesh.

> This justification of natural love as fullness of joy and life is the deepest thought in Donne's love-poems, far deeper and sincerer than the Platonic conceptions of the affinity and identity of souls.[26]

Grierson, however, observes the possibility that Donne may not have achieved that ideal Platonic 'marriage of true minds' either in life or in his poetry apart from the getting of "pictures in our eyes". A close analysis of poems celebrating the unity of the lovers shows them as testimony to the corporeal basis of communion, while yet quite apart from mere sensuous consciousness. *The Extasie* has it thus:

> Our hands were firmely cimented
> With a fast balme, which thence did spring,
> Our eye-beams twisted, and did thred
> Our eyes, upon one double string;
> So to'entergraft our hands, as yet
> Was all the meanes to make us one,
> And pictures in our eyes to get
> Was all our propagation.

In *The good-morrow* their love, which is so exalted as to be "all pleasures fancies", and which excludes all the worlds besides, needs "one little roome" for "an every where" in which to assemble the two hemispheres of their eyes in a passionate embrace. What we must infer from these is that the united souls of lovers have no ethereal universe other than what their bodies take for granted. Grierson may not agree with Courthope that Donne has demolished the 'fine Platonic edifice' of idealized love[27] in his poetry, insisting that Donne has, through the wide range of his experience, come to realize a new philosophy of love which is less dualistic and ascetic than that of Dante; there is, however, little indication in his poems that the transcendental moment of lover' spiritual union is sustained long enough not to feel the need of tangible experience to authenticate it. A.J. Smith is of this view when, discussing two of Donne's most Platonic poems *The Relique* and *The Undertaking*, he says,

> there's no hint of transcendence or of ideal forms; if they pose an ideal for lovers, it's certainly not a disembodied ideal.[28]

Without the moral bias that the word 'sex' has to come to earn, A.J. Smith may be understood as saying that Donne conceives of love as a harmonious duality of spirit and flesh when he looks upon Donne as "a poet for whom love is intrinsically sexual."[29] Leo Spitzer, on the other hand, believes that Donne

> was more intimately convinced of the reality and beauty of the spiritual union than of the necessity of the body for that union.[30]

This pro-Platonic view is the corollary of his preference of interpreting the word 'forbeare' as meaning 'endure, to tolerate', in opposition to Legouis' meaning which is 'restrain, control', as well as his equating to 'bodies' the plane of natural existence, and not the act of sex. Yet, this view might gain less support than may the alternative view that whatever degree of 'extasie' the lovers' souls do attain, the same has been by virtue of their physical existence, which is the sum total of the argument of *The Extasie*.

The lovers, mutually attracted to each other by their love, sat on a bank silently, their hands firmly gripping together in a passionate lock. Their searching eyes met, and these too were locked on to each other as if they had been threaded with the beams of their self-seeing sights. Their bodies were, so to say, united innocently. In such a rapturous moment, each had forgotten self in the contemplation of the other in a perfect 'marriage of true minds', while the bodies passively assume statuesque posture. One versed in soul's language and a perfect Platonic lover too (were such a person be and were he present there to overhear the souls conversing) would have learnt new lesson in love for his own edification. And this is what the souls said—their souls' *extasie* on going out of their bodies, had—

> revealed to them the true nature of their love. They had had no idea what had moved them to love so purely that sex did not occur to them. Like a violet

> transplanted, their love, which had suffered deprivation in isolation, had found the secret of their joy's fullness in the interdependence of their two loves whose growth their immortal souls fed—souls that do not undergo change like mortal flesh and blood.

Had Donne been a Platonist the poem could well have ended here. That it did not, gives occasion to speculate upon the bearing the rest of the poem has on the whole. As for the contested meaning of 'forbear', its bearing on the earlier reference to 'our bodies' seems to suggest a reproach for having so long (i.e., all day) forgotten their bodies. How could they have been so soul-selfishly indulgent as to deprive them of their fair share in love? For they are the planet whose living souls they are; and thus they are obliged to their bodies for their very essence, as souls are begotten by the labours of blood in the subtle knot of pure lovers' souls indwelling their bodies.

The union of lovers must now change its locale, namely, to their bodies; since 'prophane men' 'will no faith bestow' on such a love which can 'forget the He and shee'. And since only a mystic in love can perceive and appreciate love in the abstract union of souls, love must descend to the body for it to be understood by men of cruder vision. And when the soul returns to the body, so must love take form in the woman's "moving" body or remain a "Some lovely glorious nothing" incapable relation or communication.

Having seen and heard the progress of the lovers' souls, the observer is given the assurance that their love would hardly undergo any change (implied—for the worse) by their union in the flesh.

In the light of Donne's more liberal exercise on the incarnate love in his *Elegies*, Leo Spitzer's distaste for what he calls "Gallic worldly wisdom" in Legouis's reading of the poem as a seductive invitation[31] looks more like a moral predilection than an analytical conviction. It may not be possible to locate particular biographical incidents to illustrate a pertinent idea that Donne had had a vigorous youth for which the repentant cries of the *Holy Sonnets* are more than devotional pietism. It has been said of Tolstoy that he felt it more than his tortured conscience could do to allay his sexual vigour in his married life. What C.S. Lewis had said about Donne being troubled by the medieval sense of sinfulness of sex discussed above might have been more true of Tolstoy than of Donne whose sense of guilt appears to be more engendered by the generic sinfulness inherent in fallen human nature than by any specific act deserving divine censure. That beautiful confession of sin and prayer for divine forgiveness, *A Hymn to God the Father*, as well as the *Holy Sonnet XIX*, when placed beside the words of another dialectician, a man of unquestioned reputation, St Paul himself,

> But I see another law in my members, warring against the law of my mind, and bringing me into captivity to the law of sin which is in my members. Oh, wretched man that I am! Who shall deliver me from the body of this death? (*Romans* 7:23, 24)

will be found not to have needed particulars to call for repentant palinodes.

> Th'hydroptique drunkard, and night-scouting thiefe,
> The itchy Lecher, and selfe tickling proud
> Have the remembrance of past joyes, for reliefe
> Of coming ills. to (poore) me is allow'd
> No ease; for, long, yet vehement griefe hath beene
> Th'effect and cause, the punishment and sinne.
>
> *(Holy Sonnet III)*

But for the more religious temperament, Donne may be seen as less troubled by the sense of sinfulness of lust than Shakespeare is. Shakespeare's sense of sinning seems to emanate from the thought that his better sense or reason in love has been cheated out of its principles by the weakness of the flesh, so that he feels himself drawn towards sexual love against the will of his reason till reason itself becomes confused.

> O me, what eyes hath Love put in my head,
> Which have no correspondence with true sight!
> Or, if they have, where is my judgement fled,
> That censures falsely what they see aright?
>
> *(Sonnet 148)*

Making love, in the full modern sense, has no moral compunction in Donne's poetry. But the danger and consequence of equating sexual act with the deeper springs of love is brought out by Donne in a manner which has often been misinterpreted as a rejection or dismissal of love.[32] For Donne to reject love there must needs be another Donne who is the very picture of profligacy, the debauched unfeeling philanderer of *Communitie*, *Confined Love*, *Loves Alchymie*, and perhaps of *The Dreame* too, where women are 'fruits', 'mummy', 'Loves Myne', and morally neutral.

> And when hee hath the kernell eate,
> Who doth not fling away the shell? *(Communitie)*

One is reminded of the Wife of Bath in Chaucer's *Canterbury Tales:*

> Are birds divorc'd, or are they chidden
> If they leave their mate, or lie abroad a night?
> Beasts doe no jointures lose
> Though they new lovers choose,
> But we are made worse than those.
>
> *(Confined Love)*

In *The Dreame* she is the fire which kindles the primed torch of the poet's love. But *Twicknam garden* is the Eden whose peace is broken by the serpent love. Even the promise of love's increase in spring is foreshadowed by its own dialectical basis of false surmise and unpredictability about love's progress beginning *Loves growth*:

> I scarce beleeve my love to be so pure
> As I had thought it was,
> Because it doth endure
> Vicissitude, and season, as the grasse;
> Me thinkes I lyed all winter, when I swore,
> My love was infinite, if spring make'it more.

Love's doom is imminent as it proceeds to mistake the fruit for the tree, as the act—"gentle love deeds"—assumes the name of love and ultimately usurps the centre.

> Gentle love deeds, as blossoms on a bough,

From loves awakened root do bud out now.
If, as in water stir'd more circles bee
Produc'd by one, love such additions take,
Those like so many spheares, but one heaven make,
For, they are all concentrique unto thee;
And though each spring doe adde to love new heate,
As princes doe in times of action get
New taxes, and remit them not in peace,
No winter shall abate the springs encrease.

Such hedonism, such apostasy, is not admitted even in the Elegies where physical love is celebrated openly—*Loves Progress* (XVIII) and *Going to Bed* (XIX), poems considered too hot for inclusion in his poems published during his lifetime. Here there is no mistaking the act for the essence of love, but one is the complement of the other. And this is what C.S. Lewis finds himself incapable of accommodating: that Donne is trying to erect "the romantic conception of 'pure' passion" by making spiritual love the justification for the use of the body.[33]

There is the Donne, the romantic lover and poet, who sincerely believes in the lovers' capacity to sustain their love in spite of universal change and decay, and which is not subject to the post coitus ennui characteristic of love that takes the act too seriously. *Farewell to Love* is, after all, inevitable if the lover considers the minute of sensual euphoria yielded by love-making as all that there is in love. The shallowness of such immature love, more like the "countrey pleasures" of *The good morrow* than a rakish debauchery, is dramatically exposed by the simile of children's ephemeral fascination:

But, from late faire
His highnesse sitting in a golden Chaire,
Is not lesse cared for after three dayes
By children, then the thing which lovers so
Blindly admire, and with such worship wooe;
Being had, enjoying it decayes:
And thence,
What before pleas'd them all, takes but one sense,
And that so lamely, as it leaves behinde
A kinde of sorrowing dulnesse to the minde.

The *Elegies* in contrast deliberately immunize themselves against the stings of conventions and opinions in making the god of love the sole arbiter in the art of loving. The poet here is fresh and delights in love in accordance with what his mind finds lovable. The ecstasy of freedom assayed here is not to be fettered by man-made laws and conventions since it has been instituted by Nature itself. To Grierson, Donne's poetry as a justification of natural love in which passion unites body and soul vindicates itself as the alternative to and escape from both the courtly ascetic (and very much hypocritical) idealism and the sensuality and exaggerated cynicism of so much of Renaissance poetry.[34] What to a casual reader may appear to be a playful libertinism in literary exercise, when read in the light of the poet's not all too compromising career in love, will look more like a Miltonic pamphlet against the very institutions that have wrested the law of love and marriage from their natural guardian than a thwarted lover's tantrum of *The Canonization*. Such a poem is *Elegie XVII: Variety*. Here, beauty is justification for love, and polygamy of the eastern princes made an example of rich loving.

> How happy were our Syres in ancient times,
> Who held plurality of loves no crime!
> With them it was accounted charity
> To stirre up race of all indifferently;
>
> ... ...
>
> But since this title honour hath been us'd,
> Our weake credulity hath been abused;
> The golden laws of nature are repeald,
>
> ... ...
>
> Here love receiv'd immedicable harmes,
> And was despoiled of his daring armes.

The same plea is urged in *Confined Love*:

> Good is not good, unlesse
> A thousand it possesse,
> But doth wast with greedinesse.

The dialectics have gone too far, it seems. For 'possession' as a means solely of alleviating 'greedinesse' does not cure the itch, but ultimately leads to condemnation of woman for failure to afford sustained 'feeling' of love, but leaving

> A kinde of sorrowing dulnesse to the minde.

Emily Pearson notices this uncomfortable relegation of woman to an object of love, and by degrees to 'Mummy'.

> Woman entered into his analysis simply because she was necessary to complete the emotional experience of love between the sexes. Whether she were dark or fair, beautiful or ugly, did not matter. His interest in her depended entirely upon two things: first, she was the stimulus to the sensations of passionate love, and second, she was necessary to his interpretation of the results of that emotional experience....[35]

And that says a lot about the nature of Donne's introspective analysis of the experience of love in almost all its variety. Besides a few scattered references to his well-known affair with his wife, Ann, his poems give little scope for investigations of Donne's affair with particular women. The two opposite poles of his reaction to the experience of love, one of ecstatic transcendence of the flesh and another of full blooded, yet controlled release of sexuality, naturally pose an inconsistency, unless it were a dichotomy in the love life of the poet—the swing of the pendulum from one extreme of sensuality to another extreme of pious fears. For Donne's life with his hard-won wife had been a happy one; and his attachment to her as a husband and a lover strong enough to suggest that the poems which dismiss or reject love and women had been written before 1600. There had been ample time to have earned his reputation as 'not dissolute but very neat, a great visitor of ladies and frequenter of plays'.

Elegie XIV: *A Tale of a Citizen and his Wife* is an impish picture of cuckoldry—a euphemistic term for adultery—once gilded brightly by courtly love convention. The licentiousness of the court circle always find suitable and effective camouflage in conventional poetizing. Against such background many Elizabethan love poems which may shock Victorian sensibility would have amused the relatively sturdier sensibility of Tudor and Stuart era. It may thus appear that Donne has been unfairly judged by the standard of another age which learnt to suppress the emotions and thoughts, only to seethe below the surface and ready to erupt in more damaging psychological justifications of its sensuality. The very daring of the cuckolding in *Elegy I: Jealosie* seems naïve, if not actually innocent:

> Fond woman, which would'st have thy husband die,
> And yet complain'st of his great jealousie;
> ... ...
> O give him many thanks, he'is courteous,
> That in suspecting kindly warneth us.
> Wee must not, as wee us'd, flout openly,
> In scoffing riddles, his deformity;
> Nor at his boord together being satt,
> With words, nor touch, scarce lookes adulterate.
> Nor when he swolne, and pamper'd with great fare,
> Sits downe, and snorts, cag'd in his basket chaire,
> Must wee usurpe his owne bed any more,
> Nor kisse and play in his house, as before.
> Now I see many dangers; for that is
> His realme, his castle, and his diocesse.
> But if, as envious men, which would revile
> Their Prince, or coyne his gold, themselves exile
> Into another countrie, 'and doe it there,
> Wee play'in another house, what should we feare?

Donne never asked the propriety of such poetry as long as it is true in expressing his thoughts and feelings. Here, Donne makes the passion its own law, love its own god.[36] Woman, as Emily Pearson observes, merely serves as the slate on which he records the power of his love. She is hardly a person sharing love with him. She has no speaking part in these poems except one, in *Breake of Day*, which is the Juliet counterpart of this one-way love affair, when like Cressida she chides her man for making business an excuse for rising from her:

> Must business thee from hence remove?
> Oh, that's the worst disease of love,

> The poore, the foule, the false, love can
> Admit, but not the busied man.

To her love is not love which has more important thing in mind than love; she can love wherever she is given unreserved love, except where she is second priority.

> He which hath business, and makes love, doth doe
> Such wrong, as when a maryed man doth wooe.

It is for such sensitive awareness of women's temperament that Arthur Symons praises Donne:

> If women most conscious of their sex were ever to read Donne, they would say, He was a great lover; he understood.[37]

Understand them, he does well enough in their bliss and in their blight. From the unabashed admiration of her naked body—

> Thy body is a naturall Paradise,
> In whose selfe, unmanur'd, all pleasure lies.
>
> *(Sapho to Philaeni)*

to the bitter disillusionment in her 'Paradise'—which, in the notorious *Farewell to Love*,

> Being had, enjoying it decayes.

all that he has come to learn is that woman's tears are all false:

> Alas, hearts do not in eyes shine,
> Nor can you more judge womans thoughts by teares,
> Then by her shadow, what she weares.
>
> *(Twicknam Garden)*

and that,

> No where
> Lives a woman true, and faire.
>
> *(Song: Goe and catche a falling starre)*

"Love enjoyed is like gingerbread with the gilt off", so C.S. Lewis comments on *Farewell to Love*.[38] So long as sex is equated with love, and pleasure its essence, woman has shown her practical wisdom in *Breake of Day*. Why should not, may not man do the same? If she would change her love where she finds more devotion (perhaps more satisfaction too), he too would not be bound to one either. The essential woman is therefore not the particular 'she' bearing a name and a distinctive personality, but she of the moment whose love is true now. Her lover has no faith in her, but is willing to love her for this 'moment of time' which in reality and for all practical purposes is the only reality he knows and will ever know, and perhaps needs to know—for the next day she would be another's love. Thus in *Womans constancy* he lifts the veil of romantic illusion:

> Now thou hast lov'd me one whole day,
> To morrow when thou leav'st, what wilt thou say?
> Wilt thou then Antedate some new made vow?
> Or say that now
> We are not just those persons, which we were?

Consummation of their love has not guaranteed that their oaths of love would be kept. He accuses her of premeditating falsehood even while loving him—of a deft jugglery of time "Antedate some new made vow" to erase the very existence and reality of this moment and fill the gap with another moment of love (and so on and so on). The invisible idea this arouses of a monster nympho swallowing up an endless chain of lovers and time is not very comforting. Is she capable of sloughing off her present identity like the snake so as to be perpetually fresh and untried? The very concept (or conceit) is staggering for its relentless probing into the deepest recesses of the Freudian syndrome. On the surface, the accusation that sleep (perhaps just as sleep after one love-making renews strength to love again) releases her from this vow to make another tomorrow is not altogether free from envy.

> So lovers contracts, images of those,
> Binde but till sleep, deaths image, them unloose?
> Or, your owne end to Justifie,
> For having purpos'ed change, and falsehood: you
> Can have no way but falsehood to be true?
> Vaine lunatique, against these scapes I could
> Dispute, and conquer, if I would,
> Which I abstaine to doe,
> For by to morrow, I may thinke so too.

And the threat and invitation are real enough, provided he is willing. Parting from her for a journey he think of, what may hap:

> Sweetest love, I do not goe,
> For weariness of thee,
> Nor in hope the world can show
> A fitter Love for mee. *(Song: Sweetest Love...)*

In spite of his anger, distaste, and contempt for the bitter reality of the world of loving which is full of briars, he cannot abandon it altogether, not for the irresistible sexual impetus, but for the bright gem of true love that he sees shining among the thorns. The swaggering male chauvinism of *Communitie*,

> Change'd loves are but chang'd sorts of meat,
> And when hee hath the kernel [eate,] eate,
> Who doth not fling away the shell?

of *Elegie III: Change*,

> Women are like the Arts, forc'd unto none,
> Open to'all searchers, unpriz'd, if [unknowne.]
> ... ...
> Women are made for men, not him, nor mee.
> Foxes and goats; all beasts change when they please,
> Shall women, more hot, wily, wild then these,
> Be bound to one man...?
> ... ... Change'is the nursery
> Of musicke, joy, life, and eternity.

and the final rejection of the evanescent love afforded by woman in *Farewell to Love* should not be taken as a dismissal of the poet's experienced love of *The Anniversarie*, *the Canonization*, and *A Valediction: forbidding mourning*, where love is more an act of the will than an emotional state subject to the life of the senses.

> Dull sublunary lovers love
> (Whose soul is sense) cannot admit
> Absence, because it doth remove
> Those things which elemented it.

There is such a close similarity between *A Valediction: forbidding mourning* and Shakespeare's *Sonnet 116* that it seems Done too has expressed in these poems a love which not merely transcends, but actually modifies and glorifies the entire machinery of loving in a human being, which, un-united, expresses itself in such cynical voice of disillusioned distaste as in *Loves Alchymie*, *Twicknam Garden*, and *Farewell to Love*. And it may be wrong to suppose that Donne is unable to sustain his ideal of love which some believe is a form of Platonism sweetened with the licence of hedonism as expressed in *The Extasie* for the very reason that these two poles are mutually sustaining, in spite of the poet's claim that the observer shall see "Small change, when we're to bodies gone".

Among those who see a reluctant admission of the vulnerability of human love in a world governed by Time and mutability in Donne, Waller brings Bruno's concept of the moment (the now) as the basic unit of time and eternity to bear on Donne's affirmation of the experienced moment as the only reality. According to Bruno,

> we seize our opportunities only 'amid the changes and chances of life', for 'if there were not mutation, variety, and vicissitude, there would be nothing agreeable, nothing good, nothing pleasurable'.[39]

Waller, however, rejects D.W. Harding's suggestion that Donne's love poetry voices 'fantasies of permanence' as an escape from the pressures of mutability, and asserts the poet's willingness to be a part of the continually moving reality, for, he says,

> it is precisely because of time's passing that love exists and grows. The real fears that transitoriness, loss, and death can bring are faced clearly, and then calmly set aside.[40]

The microcosm of the lovers' unique experience, notwithstanding its exclusiveness, does not really dismiss the existence of the external universe which threatens to relegate their relationship to a mere genetic impulse. What Donne actually communicates by means of apparent exclusion in *The good-morrow* and *The Sunne rising* is the nagging realization that the unruly sun, in obedience to the 'new philosophy', insists on taking his place at the centre. And poor new man must revolve with his hours and days. The old aged sun is flattered into a pedant by new scholarship, assuming a guardian's duty to which he has been promoted from the drudgery of 'warming the world'. And love knows all too well seasons, days, and hours, as they punctuate the lovers' movements.

> Why should we rise, because 'tis light?
> Did we lie down, because 'twas night? *(Break of Day)*

> For I had rather owner bee
> Of thee one houre, then all else ever... *(A Feaver)*

> O how feeble is mans power,
> That if good fortune fall,
> Cannot adde another houre,
> Nor a lost houre recall! *(Song: Sweetest Love...)*

> And Lovers houres be full of eternity. *(The Lagacie)*

And it is this irrepressible consciousness of Time that lends additional poignancy to Donne's poems. As a man who sincerely sought comfort and stay in the experience of love which alone promised a stability so much needed to answer his increasing awareness of corruption, dissolution and decay of man's estate, his assertion of lover's sufficiency to endure and keep pace with obliterating Time appears but as a drowning man catching at straws. For even the most assured certainty of love is not above the sway of Time's autocracy, but is an integral part of its materialization. Love, therefore, he admits, is not an ethereal constancy of undiminishing light, but a motion, and a growth conditioned by Time's circumstances; And as such must endure the change and mortality of all flesh by which alone it takes life and existence. This is the topic of *A Lecture upon the Shadow*:

> Except our loves at this noone stay,
> We shall new shadows make the other way.
> ... ...

If our loves faint, and westwardly decline;
To me thou, falsely, thine,
And I to thee mine actions shall disguise.

The end of love, though, often comes before the lovers' death: infidelity desperately masking its actions where no love exists any more to take offence! But as long as love is mutually taken for granted, it makes an everlasting day, not by arresting time or by escaping from it, but by a continuous sort of constancy in the ever present 'now':

All Kings, and all their favorites,
All glory of honors, beauties, wits,
The Sun it selfe, which makes times, as they passe,
Is elder by a yeare, now, then it was
When thou and I first one another saw:
All other things, to their destruction draw,
Only our love hath no decay;
This, no to morrow hath, nor yesterday,
Running it never runs from us away,
But truly keeps his first, last, everlasting day.

(The Anniversarie)

Is this a true and stable experience which can neutralize the crippling effect of Time's passage over man's aspirations? Or is it a mere 'fantasies of permanence', an escape from the 'contemptus mundi' of his time—'corruptio optimi pessima':

And soonest our best men with thee doe goe.

(Holy Sonnet X)

and his morbid fear of the world's physical disintegration? Donne's haunting obsession with universal instability in a way renders his works apt to be interpreted as sceptical of the possibility and worth of virtue in a world doomed to progressive corruption and ultimate disintegration consequent upon the Fall of our first parents, especially of the woman.

There is no health; Physitians say that wee,
At best, enjoy but a neutralitie.
And can there bee worse sicknesse, then to know
That we are never well, nor can be so?

Wee are borne ruinous....
For that first marriage was our funerall:
One woman at one blow, then kill'd us all,
And singly, one by one, they kill us now.
We doe delightfully our selves allow
To that consumption; and profusely blinde,
Wee kill our selves to propagate our kinde.
And yet we do not that; we are not men.

(The First Anniversarie)

To say that in *The first Anniversarie*, the life and death of Elizabeth Drury exemplifies the inevitability of corruption and the insurmountability of 'a sense of sin and contemptus mundi' and at the same time claim that she is the transfiguration of the 'celestial potential of man'[41] rather makes the transcendental potential of man weak and unconvincing. That the spiritual aspect is not Donne's preoccupation in this poem is suggested by Sukanta Chaudhuri, when he says that the life and death of Elizabeth Drury "inspires not triumph but humility", and that,

> The potential perfection of man, thwarted by the basic circumstances of his being, casts his actual corruption into deeper gloom.[42]

The state of man suffers not merely decentralization and mortification of his divine nature, but a shrinking, a physical diminution, not as quickly but not unlike that of Milton's fallen angels thronging Pandemonium. The picture is not that of Hamlet's disillusioned dissection of the humanistic idealization of man—godlike man reduced to quintessence of dust—but a kind of retro-evolutionary process by which post-lapsarian man has degenerated from a giant multicentenarian to a sickly pigmy consumed by his own lust and intemperance.

Where is this mankinde now? who lives to age,
Fit to be made Methusalem his page?
Alas, we scarce live long enough to try
Whether a true made clocke run right, or lie.

This living corruption affects the body as well as the mind:

And as our bodies, so our mindes are crampt:

> 'Tis shrinking, not close weaving that hath thus
> In minde, and body both bedwarfed us. (II.152-54)

It may, at this juncture, be asked whether Donne is personally more involved than Hamlet in their respective rejections of man's intrinsic worth. In Hamlet's wounded judgement man is a dichotomy of virtue and vice, of godlike intelligence and beauty yet, a mere lump of clay, the majestic empyrean firmament with the golden sun turned to a "foul and pestilent congregation of vapours". In truth, Hamlet has lost all faith in existence when the highest and noblest example of man he knows,

> Where every god did seem to set his seal,
> To give the world assurance of a man. (III.4.61, 62)

his own father and the love that had flowered between him and his mother who

> would hang on him
> As if increase of appetite had grown
> By what it fed on. (I.2.143, 144)

crumble to dust and forgotten in the heat of incestuous embrace. To him to exist means to negate meaning and purpose in life; to remain a moral chameleon capable of saying

> there is nothing either good or bad, but thinking makes it so. (II.2.248)

He does not reject the humanist's paragon of creation; but he has lost the sweet taste of it in his life. He refuses to be a part of this ambivalent world. He rejects even Ophelia for being a woman in whom love is betrayed, and he would not trust his love with her or any woman. He has nothing to live for; and he takes his death without fear or regret, but as a blissful rest from the 'harsh world'.

Donne begins from a less exalted premise of admitting the inevitability of the world's corruption as a logical and natural consequence of man's action. There is no way by which man can escape, short of dying.

> Thou seest a Hectique feaver hath got hold
> Of the whole substance, not to be contrould,

And that thou hast but one way, not t'admit
The worlds infection, to be none of it.

(The First Anniversarie)

To be human has no more divine dignity than to be the smallest organism of soulless animalcule to which Faustus would fain be changed. Man has not merely lost his pre-eminence in the universal hierarchy of Correspondence; ruin has worked upon his entire nature which is a part of the disintegrating system.

This man, whom God did wooe, and loth t'attend
Till man came up, did downe to man descend,
This man, so great, that all that is, is his,
Oh what a trifle and poore thing he is!

(The First Anniversarie)

The regular eulogizing of Miss Elizabeth Drury in the two Anniversaries as the figure of all perfections due to pre-lapsarian man concludes with the futility of her virtue in the context of a centreless universe in which 'correspondence' is a misnomer, for,

So, of the Starres which boast that they doe runne
In Circle still, none ends where he begun.

(The First Anniversarie)

By attributing to Elizabeth Drury the very essence and quality of an immanent spirit of God, and making her the epitome of spiritual perfection in human form, Donne seems to make her, not just 'the Idea of a Woman',[43] but the archetype of the Original Woman (as she would be, if only she were) untainted by her disobedience. Yet the poem appears to tip the balance against what Louis L. Martz regards as the central theme: the true end of man.[44] And the genius of the poet tends more towards confirming the hopeless state of man than towards imbuing the latter's responsibility to restore the original image in accordance with the view of St. Bernard that that image of God in Man is indestructible, however distorted or maimed.[45] The transcendence of the world's disease by Elizabeth is by no means universal. Therefore, she fails to redeem mankind, even if the poem has been an attempt to that end by typifying the Christ image—mainly because the poet had more reasons to preserve the individuality of Elizabeth Drury by freeing her from the corrupting elements that make up the body, than to let her purifying essence transform its earthly tenement. The strain is again felt when 'shee', by her death, betrays the hope she inspired.

> She, of whom th'Ancients seem'd to prophesie,
> When they call'd vertues by the name of *shee*;
> Shee in whom vertue was so much refin'd,
> That for Allay unto so pure a minde
> Shee tooke the weaker Sex; shee that could drive
> The poysonous tincture, and the staine of *Eve*,
> Out of her thoughts, and deeds; and purifie
> All, by a true religious Alchymie;
> Shee, shee is dead; shee's dead: when thou knowest this,
> Thou knowest how poore a trifling thing man is.

The heroic assertion of the *Songs and Sonnets* on the validity of the experience of love has to be valued against this brooding sense of total futility. The only way to any meaning to life is removal from the entire system by separation of the immortal and the mortal parts of man by 'second birth',

> That is, thy death; for though the soul of man
> Be got when man is made, 'tis borne but than
> When man doth die; our body's as the wombe,
> And, as a Mid-wife, death directs it home.

This is not an assertion of life as we understand in a conceptual manner, nor is it a validation of man's intrinsic worth as conceived in the mind of Renaissance humanists, if we are to understand by *humanism*, the reliance on and the cultivation of human reason and talents to attain fulfillment in life as opposed to the view that man's pursuit of self-fulfillment must come mainly through spiritual exercise and mortification of the flesh, including renunciation of the world's good.

> And that except thou feed (not banquet) on
> The supernatural food, Religion,

> Thy better Growth grows withered, and scant;
> Be more then man, or thou'rt lesse than an Ant.

In this vision of universal curse and anticipation of a transcendent existence in a resurrected life the Pauline thesis of universal iniquity and resurrection may have been a significant base. But it is difficult to ascertain to what extent the word 'identification' is used by Prof. Hughes when positing that Donne "will adopt St Paul as a type of himself".[46] It is true that significant passages from St Paul's *Epistles to the Romans* find echoes and direct application:

> For all have sinned, and come short of the glory of God. (3:23)

> For the earnest expectation of the creation waiteth for the manifestation of the sons of God. (8:19)

This, however, is in the early stage of Donne's poetic career. Yet it is interesting to evaluate the extent to which Donne has been infused with Scriptures to emerge later as the best preacher of his time, and the penitent poet of some of the most confessed *Holy Sonnets*.

A comprehensive study of Donne's inside career to this effect has been made by Richard E. Hughes in *The Progress of the Soul: The Interior Career of John Donne*, written over a period of thirteen years. There Prof Hughes has drawn a clear path of Donne's development from a mood "very like *existential disappointment*"[47] to "a world of fantasy where the ambiguities and the paradoxes are solved by the unitive experience of love"[48] which he created in his love poetry, and thence to the final and ultimate resolution of the existential debate in the substitution of Christ for "the woman who has failed him as the guide to Paradise".[49] This is a beautiful summing up of a poet's otherwise divergent streams of poetic inspiration. But to call what Donne has found to be a tangible reality of happiness in love a mere fantasy is to make that worthwhile experience subservient to another dimension alien to it. For there is no way we can equate the lovers' sense of bliss with the Paradise offered by Christ. The nearest Donne comes to identifying lover's pleasures with the word 'Paradise' seems to be with tongue in cheek, conscious of an innocent blasphemy:

> In such white robes, heaven's Angels us'd to be
> Receaved by men; Thou Angel bringst with thee
> A heaven like Mahomets paradise.... *(Elegie XIX)*

It appears not unfeasible, but easily misleading, to seek a definitive and coherent 'philosophy of love' in the entire works of Donne. And to emphasize some poems at the expense of others, as Phillip Mallet thinks,

> would obviously be improper, it seems better not to look for a carefully composed 'lecture...in love's philosophy', but to accept that Donne expressed different attitudes in different poems according to the mood of the moment.[50]

It is indeed very attractive to find Donne purified of his 'prophane Love', and filled with a holier but less corporeal Love; Donne "the simulacrum of modern man",[51] the perpetual seeker after wholeness.[52] And so it would seem that Donne was experimenting with human love as a "prolegomenon to divine love", strongly supported by the sermons of the poet himself.[53] And to further identify the "elusive" woman of the *Songs and Sonets* with "the apprehended light announced by St John",[54] and the lover's total satisfaction of *The good-morrow* with the anticipation of the Church Triumphant in *Holy Sonnet XVIII*, is to take no little critical licence.

Donne loved, and wrote upon it. His poetry is not about Love as a philosophical concept; it is the record of his loving and his private discursions on his intensely passionate and frustrated experience. His poetry deviates sharply from other love-poetry for its significant refusal to recognize any external motive for loving save his insistent need to be united in flesh and will. And if at one point he is aware of an empty bliss, at another point he finds rewarding achievement of an unqualified sense of unity which even transcends the [physical means by which it is attained, as in *The Undertaking*:

> But he who lovelinesse within

Hath found, all outward loathes,
For he who colour loves, and skinne,
Loves but their oldest clothes.

If, as I have, you also doe
Vertue'attir'd in woman see,
And dare love that, and say so too,
And forget the Hee And Shee.

Like a man thrown upon the world against his will, Donne revolted against the system which had put him upon the rack of subsistence, even as he was simultaneously enraptured and mystified by the potential he found in man and woman to rise above the sordid business of finding a suitable livelihood. Even while living on top of the world Donne never relaxes his intellectual grip on the world, but feels it moving. The lovers' bed is no Arden where "Time travels in divers paces with divers persons". Time with Donne travels impersonally with the movement of the Earth, and no 'microcosmizing' may lock out the prying Sun, the universal Time-keeper.

But Time can really be made subservient to the lovers as the means by which love is evaluated. From the sarcastic philandering of *Loves Vsury* to the ardent affirmation of constancy in love through Time's revolutions in *The Anniversarie*, Donne reveals an inveterate consciousness of Time so that every act he describes in his poems comes alive as if it were a direct confession. We are conscious of a definite past, present, and future here. At times Donne makes a playful show of his ability to 'eclipse' time as an external order subject to the will of man's mind.

Love, all alike, no season knows, nor clime,
Nor houres, dayes, moneths, which are the rags of time.
Thy beames, so reverend, and strong
Why shouldst thou think?
I could eclipse and cloud them with a winke,
But that I would not lose her sight so long.

(The Sunne Rising)

The 'microcosm' here does not mean seclusion from the macrocosm for the very reason that the lovers are more aware of time than if they had not loved. It is their heightened awareness of life and sharpened sensibility that give them the microcosmic panorama of life as their love reveals to them. It is in such arrested moments of time that even a career-loving Donne can say,

> All honor's mimique; All wealth alchimie,

just as Antony raises his love for Cleopatra above the glory of an Empire:

> Let Rome in Tiber melt, and the wide arch
> Of the rang'd empire fall! Here is my space.
>
> (I.1.33, 34)

Donne was ever conscious of the vulnerability of virtue in a fallen world; and the love he asserted is not without the inevitable consequence of seclusion and deprivation of that world where love is known simply as a commodity. It is ironical that Donne's search for a truly transcending love was at last rewarded by his commitment to the Church he had all along avoided. Yet it must be admitted that even before he confessed a love that identifies itself with the love of God for a sinful world, Donne has confessed to a love that does not depend on mere externals and physical togetherness, a love that transcends time and space, love which,

> Inter-assured of the mind,
> Care lesse, eyes, lips, and hands to misse.
>
> (*A Valediction: Forbidding Mourning*)

But even when he invokes a more sustaining love—"th'Eternall root/Of true Love"—his love for these below happens to be the occasion:

> O, if thou car'st not whom I love
> Alas, thou lov'st not mee.
>
> (*A Hymne to Christ, at the Authors last going into Germany*)

And to express his newly acquired love for God, Donne has only the usual vocabulary of human courtship:

> That I may rise, and stand, o'erthrow me, and bend

Your force, to breake, blowe, burn and make me new.
... ...
Divorce mee, 'untie, or breake that knot againe,
Take mee to you, imprison mee, for I
Except you' enthrall mee, never shall be free,
Nor ever chast, except you ravish mee.

(*Holy Sonnet XIV*)

The essence of love, whether of woman or of God, is the same to Donne. He says in his Sermon:

> Love is a Possessory Affection... it delivers over him that loves into the possession of that he loves; it is a transmutatory Affection, it changes him that loves, into the very nature of that that he loves, and he is nothing else.[55]

How near, one may say, this comes to resemble Keats's description of the Poetical character which has been used to illustrate Shakespeare's treatment of love! And such is the man whose capacity to love and whose ideas of loving may not be circumscribed by a woman's arms, but must take in all men and women in the sweep of the compass. What man can do more in the name of love than to be able to say—

> No Man is an Iland, intire of it selfe; euery man is a peece of the continent, a part of the maine; if a Clod bee whashed away by the Sea, Europe is the lesse, as well as if a Promontorie were, as well as if a Manor of thy friends, or of thine owne were; Any Man's death diminishes me, because I am inuolued in Mankinde.
>
> *Devotions upon Emergent Occasions*[56]

as Donne has?

NOTES

1. Waller, *English Poetry of the Sixteenth Century*, p. 237.
2. Stanzas from the Grand Chartreuse.
3. George Williamson, *A Reader's Guide to the Metaphysical Poets*, Thames & Hudson, 1977, p. 40.
4. Murray Roston, *The Soul of Wit*, Oxford, 1974, p. 14.
5. *Infirm Glory*, p. 112.
6. "A thought to Donne was an experience; it modified his sensibility." *The Metaphysical Poets* (1921).

7. *The Metaphysical Poets*, Fortnightly Review (1899), reprinted in Casebook series, ed. Gerald Hammond, Macmillan, 1974, p. 81.
8. *Donne's Love Poetry*, an essay which forms part of the introduction to *The Poems of John Donne*, 1912; also in *John Donne: A Collection of Critical Essays*, Twentieth Century Views, ed. Helen Gardner, Prentice Hall, India, 1979, pp. 23-24.
9. See Ref. 19 of Chapter 1.
10. *The Language of Paradox: The Canonization*, part of the first chapter of *The Well-wrought Urn*, NY, 1947, London 1949. Here from *Twentieth Century Views*, ed. Helen Gardner, p. 102.
11. A.J. Smith, *Donne: Songs and Sonnets*, Edward Arnold, 1964, repr. 1978, p. 21.
12. *Ibid.*, p. 22.
13. G. Williamson, *op. cit.*, p. 44.
14. 'The Love Poetry of John Donne, A Reply to Mr. C.S. Lewis', in *Seventeenth Century Studies Presented to Sir Herbert Grierson*. Here from John Donne's Poetry—Authoritative Texts Criticism, sel. & ed., A.L. Clements, W.W. Norton & Co. Inc., NY, 1966, p. 166.
15. Donne, *The Will.*
16. *John Donne: A Reconsideration*, Helen (ed.) *op. cit.*, p. 77.
17. *Ibid.*, p. 80.
18. *Ibid.*, p. 17.
19. *The Songs and Sonets of John Donne*, Theodore Redpath, (ed.), Methuen, 1976, p. 130.
20. Pearson, *op. cit.*, p. 230.
21. *Twentieth Century Views*—John Donne, ed. Helen Gardner, p. 92.
22. *Richard E., Hughes*, *The Progress of the Soul: The Interior Career of John Donne*, NY, 1968, p. 7.
23. H.J.C., Grierson, ed. *Donne: Poetical Works*, p. xviii.
24. *English Poetry in the Renaissance: A Study in the Adaptation of Literary Convention in Metaphysical Poets*, ed. K.N. Sinha, Kalyani, 1980, p. 13.
25. *Donne's Love Poetry*, Helen Gardner, ed., *op. cit.*, p. 33.
26. *Loc. cit.*
27. *Op. cit.*, p. 23.
28. "The Dismissal of Love", in *John Donne: Essays in Celebration*, ed. A.J. Smith, Methuen, London, 1972, p. 130.
29. *Ibid.*, p. 131
30. The Extasie—A Method of Interpreting Literature, 1949, Casebook ed., G. Hammond, p. 124.
31. *Ibid.*, p. 125.
32. *The Dismissal of Love*, *op. cit.*, p. 121. Also Pearson, *op. cit.*, p. 230.
33. Gardner, ed. *op. cit.*, p. 92.
34. *Ibid.*, pp. 32-33.
35. *Op. cit.*, p. 223.
36. Helen Gardner, *The Religious Poetry of John Donne*, *op. cit.*, p. 135.
37. *The Metaphysical Poets*, Casebook, ed., Hammond, p. 80.
38. Gardner, ed., *op. cit.*, p. 95.

39. Waller, *op. cit.*, p. 248.
40. *Ibid.*, pp. 247-48.
41. *Infirm Glory*, pp. 99-100.
42. *Ibid.*, p. 100
43. To Ben Jonson's objection that "Donne's *Anniversary* was profane and full of blasphemies," Donne replied "that he described the idea of a Woman and not as she was." *Conversation with Drummond*, Ben Jonson, *Works*, ed. Herford and Simpson, i.133, quoted in Louis L. Martz, *John Donne in Meditation*, Gardner, ed., *op. cit.*, p. 154.
44. *Loc. cit.*, p. 164.
45. *Ibid.*, p. 163.
46. Hughes, *op. cit.*, p. 127.
47. *Ibid.*, p. 71.
48. *Ibid.*, p. 79.
49. *Ibid.*, p. 127.
50. *Notes on Selected Poems: John Donne*, York Notes, Longman, 1983, 1985, p. 96.
51. Hughes, *op. cit.*, p. 281.
52. Implied in Hughes, *op. cit.*, p. 279: "Man—of all ages and cultures—is confronted with the solution of one and the same question: the question of how to overcome separateness, how to achieve union, how to transcend one's own individual life and find atonement." Erich Fromme, *The Art of Loving*.
53. *Ibid.*, p. 272.
54. *Ibid.*, p. 270.
55. Sermon (1617), *Sermons*, ed. C.R. Potter and E.M. Simpson, Berkeley, 1953-62.
56. Elizabeth Savage, ed. *Salzburg*, p. 122.

5

Summing up

Be cheerful, sir
Our revels now are ended.

—*The Tempest*

It is not to be unexpected, yet comforting to find Prospero mistaken in guessing the cause of Ferdinand's 'dismay' at his own display of "some passion" of which even his daughter says,

> Never till this day
> Saw I him touch'd with anger so distemper'd.
>
> (IV.1.144f)

Ferdinand is not dismayed, as assumed by Prospero, by the 'revels' on which the latter delivers an apocalyptic sermon. It is tempting to see in this outburst Shakespeare's view of life, as in several other serious and often poignant speeches in other plays which do not always present identical views. This 'insubstantial pageant' speech echoing *Sonnet 64* and Hamlet's dying words, as we know, is just an excuse and a camouflage for his vexation at his recollection of the "foul conspiracy of the beast Caliban and his confederates against my life". If this were a world-view, it is hardly one that should make an expectant groom 'cheerful'.

> Our revels now are ended. These our actors,
> As I foretold you, were all spirits, and
> Are melted into air, into thin air;

And, like the baseless fabric of this vision,
The cloud-capp'd towers, the gorgeous palaces,
The solemn temples, the great globe itself,
Yea, all which it inherit, shall dissolve,
And, like this insubstantial pageant faded,
Leave not a rack behind. We are such stuff
As dreams are made on; and our little life
Is rounded with a sleep.

(IV.1.148-158)

Yet it is a good lesson, the only lesson of eternal validity. Its very inconsistency with the situation lends it urgency. It is the sign of a man growing beyond the confines of a narrow life that he can acknowledge the truth of sudden switches of posture and utterance. Prospero's sudden inconsistent posturings have a lesson for Ferdinand. In Donne too, the same inconsistency is felt when the poet seeks the eternal in the temporal experience of love.

The entire works of Shakespeare and Donne may be seen as a drama of human conflict between consciousness and unconscious environments. This varied drama of awakened human consciousness quickens our sense of a vestige of the divine in fallen man yearning to assume the lost essence. There are more direct expressions of this yearning in Vaughan, Wordsworth and Tennyson: what we call 'intimations of immortality'. This is not to say that Shakespeare or Donne is chiefly concerned with the metaphysical problems of life, as the obvious truth is that both are concerned with man's preoccupation with his conscience. For to live, for a truly *living* person, is to be conscious; and consciousness is possible only in relation to others and environments.

A history of ideas mainly records the reasoned thoughts of men who have developed their understanding of life through a life-time of study and observation, with experiments, if needed. But the thoughts and feelings of ordinary men and women have always been expressed and recorded in songs and stories. Both Shakespeare and Donne had ample exposures to the pulse of life and ideas of their time as it appears from the direct and vivid manner of their treatment of love.

It was a fast moving epoch: the wheel of fortune spun madly without reason or justice—often at the whims of an unstable political system or as mere coincidences. Man was a chaff of life blown hither and thither by accidents of time. The 'whirligig of time' seemed to turn at the will of a depraved Machiavelli. No 'deux ex machina' descends on the Shakespearean stage to assert external providence, but ugly Nemesis with impeccable memory feeding on human folly and vices. It was an age of tired efforts. King Henry IV, perhaps the only honest politician, admits to being helpless against the current of history:

O, God! that one might read the book of fate,
And see the revolution of the times

... ...

The happiest youth, viewing his progress through,
What perils past, what crosses to ensue,
Would shut the book and sit him down and die.

(Hen. IV Pt. 2-III.1.45-56)

The poet too is tired, and says so in *Sonnet 66*:

Tir'd with all these, for restful death I cry:

only to realize that,

...to die, I leave my love alone.

The same discovery of Love's power is made by Donne in *The Sunne Rising*, where the 'Busie old foole' impersonating the wheel of moving history could well be dispensed with by 'a wink' but for the constant image of Love. Instead of being a means of escape devised by man, love is revealed as a concrete essence of time itself, so that escape from life and time is escape from love too. Eliot's assertion of the pervasive power of time makes sense in the context of love in Shakespeare and Donne:

But only in time can the moment in the rose-garden,
The moment in the arbour where the rain beat,
The moment in the draughty church at smokefall

Be remembered; involved with past and future.
Only through time time is conquered. *(Burnt Norton)*

But, as we have seen, the vision of love imperiled by time in the works of Shakespeare and Donne is stamped with the irreducible singularity of their genius. Love is esoteric for Donne. True lovers constitute a kind of priesthood and they have their exclusive arcane or secrets to which the rest of humanity are aliens.

When Donne talks of the growth and effects of love, he is talking of a phenomenon confined to the lovers. Love is a peculiarly private and personal experience with no visible bearings on the larger society. This is true even when the teeming life of the world around is felt in the poems. Shakespeare, on the contrary, sees love as both inward and outward looking, having transforming effects on life and society.

Love in Shakespeare is at once a vital inwardness and an inclusive extroversion. It not only touches and brings into play the plenitude of the lover's heart and mind but simultaneously works towards a cathartic purification, a togetherness, understanding and unification in the wider world. While it sweeps the lovers into each other's arms, its inherent outward-looking and altruistic impulse builds bridges where enmity and misunderstanding have created gulfs of separation. One has only to look at what the love-impelled Rosalind, Portia, Viola and Cordelia, among others, succeed in accomplishing in the face of the 'slings and arrows of outrageous fortune'. And one needs to take into account what Florizel and Perdita come round to achieving by off-setting and finally transforming the adversities of circumstances, i.e., the daunting accidents of time. Romeo and Juliet die, but the story of their tempestuous love is not over before rebuilding the disrupted society; in other words, before bringing the Montagues and the Capulets together. Antony and Cleopatra die but their tale is not finished before Octavius has paid his memorable tribute to Cleopatra who looks unvanquished by death, Time's scourge:

...but she looks like sleep,
As she would catch another Antony
In her strong toil of grace. (V.2.344-45)

and before his magnanimous recognition of the time-transcending luster of their love:

She shall be buried by her Antony:
No grave upon the earth shall clip in it
A pair so famous. (V.2.356-58)

These are Shakespeare's ways of suggesting love's intransigent answer to the challenge of time and mutability. They constitute not only man's bulwark of defence but his gesture of triumph.

Keats speaks of the world as a "vale of soul-making", meaning thereby that true soul-hood is to be achieved by consciously opposing the resources of the spirit to the challenge of time and circumstances. Shakespeare and, if to a lesser degree, Donne seem to be suggesting the same truth, when they see and make us see in love the power to bear infinite pain and suffering, the power of fortitude and growth. Its growth is such that

No winter shall abate the springs encrease.

(Donne: Loves Growth)

Both Shakespeare's and Donne's dramatization of love would seem to arise from a direct and immediate experience, so that one can sense the tang of actuality about the vividness of love's manifestation. The treatment is so full-blooded and undoctrinaire that modern man, shorn of all philosophical and religious support, can see in it an un-disguised mirror of his own agony and triumph.

Bibliography

1. Texts on Medieval and Renaissance Literary Works

Chaucer, Geoffrey, *The Canterbury Tales*, ed. A.C. Cawley, E.P. Dutton & Co., NY, 1975.

Donne, John, *Poetical Works*, ed. H.J.C. Grierson, Oxford, 1929. *Songs and Sonnets*, ed. Theodore Redpath, Methuen (London), 1959.

Marlowe, Christopher, *Works*, ed. C.F. Tucker Brooke, OUP, 1910, 1969.

Shakespeare, William, *Complete Works*, ed. P. Alexander, Collins (London), 1951. *Sonnets*, ed. W.G. Ingram and Theodore Redpath, Hodder and Stoughton, (London), 1964.

Spenser, Edmund, *Poetical Works*, ed. E. de Selincourt and J.C. Smith, OUP, 1975.

Stone, Brian, tr., *Medieval English Verse*, Penguin, Hammondsworth, 1964.

2. Works bearing on Renaissance Philosophy and Literature

Chaudhuri, Sukanta, *Infirm Glory: Shakespeare and the Renaissance Image of Man*, Clarendon (Oxford), 1981.

Copleston, S.J. Frederick, *A History of Philosophy*, Vol. 3, Image Books, NY, 1963.

Tillyard, E.M.W., *The Elizabethan World Picture*, Penguin, 1975.

Waller, Gary F., *The Strong Necessity of Time*, The Hague, 1976.

3. Works bearing on treatment of the themes of Love, Time and Mutability in the works of Shakespeare and Donne

Bennet, Joan, "*The Love Poetry of John Donne: A Reply to Mr. C.S. Lewis*", in *Seventeenth Century Studies Presented to Sir Herbert Grierson*, Oxford 1938, ed. J. Dover Wilson.

Brooks, Cleanth, *The Language of Paradox: The Canonization*, in 'The Well-wrought Urn' (London 1949).

Eliot, T.S., "*The Metaphysical Poets*", in *Selected Essays*, Faber, London, 1932.

Grierson, H.J.C., *Cross Currents in English Literature of the Seventeenth Century*, London, 1929.

Hughes, R.E., *Progress of the Soul: The Interior Career of John Donne*, NY., 1968.

Lever, J.W., *The Elizabethan Love-Sonnet*, London, 1956.

Levin, Harry, *Shakespeare and the Revolution of the Times*, OUP, NY, 1976.

Lewis, C.S., *The Discarded Image: An Introduction to Medieval and Renaissance Literature*, Cambridge, 1964. "*Donne and Love Poetry*" *in the Seventeenth Century* in *Seventeenth Century Studies Presented to Sir Herbert Grierson*, 1938.

Lyons, Charles R., *Shakespeare and the Ambiguity of Love's Triumph*, The Hague, 1971. *Reason and Love in Shakespeare*—A Selective Study, Machilipattam, 1977.

Mahood, M.M., "*Love's Confined Doom*" in *Shakespeare Survey*, 15, ed. A. Nicoll, 1962.

Pearson, Lu Emily, *Elizabethan Love Convention*, George Allen & Unwin, 1966.

Ram, Alur Janaki, *Perspective on Shakespeare*, Jaipur, 1987.

Spencer, Theodore, *Shakespeare and the Nature of Man*, Macmillan, 1971.

Stewart, J.I.M., *Character and Motive in Shakespeare*, 1949.

Turner, Frederick, *Shakespeare and the Nature of Time*, Oxford, 1971.

Waller, Gary F., *English Poetry of the Sixteenth Century*, Longman, NY, 1986.

Index